ABOUT THE AUTHORS

Kieran Keohane is Senior Lecturer in Sociology at National University of Ireland, Cork (UCC). He has taught at the universities of York, Toronto; Carleton, Ottawa; and Trent. He is the author of *Symptoms of Canada: An Essay on the Canadian Identity* (University of Toronto Press, 1997), as well as numerous articles on Irish identity and cultural sociology. His work has been published in *Canadian Review of Sociology and Anthropology; Irish Journal of Sociology; Irish Sociological Chronicles; Philosophy and Social Criticism; Journal of Political Ideologies; Theory, Culture and Society;* and *Cultural Politics.*

Carmen Kuhling is Lecturer in Sociology and Women's Studies at the University of Limerick (UL). She has taught in Trent University and University of Regina in Canada, and at NUI Cork and Trinity College in Ireland. She is the author of *The New Age Ethic and the Spirit of Postmodernity* (Hampton Press, New Jersey, 2004), as well as a number of papers on cultural sociology, cultures of resistance, and Irish and Canadian identity. Her work has appeared in the *Irish Journal of Sociology, Ephemera, Space and Culture* and *Borderlines.*

COLLISION CULTURE

Transformations in Everyday Life in Ireland

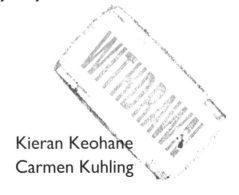

Kieran Keohane
Carmen Kuhling

The Liffey Press

Published by
The Liffey Press
Ashbrook House
10 Main Street, Raheny,
Dublin 5, Ireland
www.theliffeypress.com

A catalogue record of this book is
available from the British Library.

ISBN 1-904148-61-1

Printed in Spain by GraphyCems.

CONTENTS

This book is dedicated to our children Ilyana and Ronan,
who embody the utopian possibilities of collision culture

ACKNOWLEDGEMENTS

Most of the essays that comprise this book were originally published elsewhere, as follows: "Collision culture: road traffic accidents and the experience of accelerated modernisation in Ireland" (co-authored with Mervyn Horgan), *Irish Journal of Sociology*, Vol. 12.1, 2003; "Understanding Irish Suicides" (co-authored with Derek Chambers) and "Case studies in the localisation of the global: Celebrity in contemporary Irish culture", both in M. Peillon and M. Corcoran (eds.) (2002), *Ireland Unbound*, Irish Sociological Chronicles No. 3, Dublin, IPA Press; "Irish consumerism as collective gift relations" in M. Peillon and M. Corcoran (eds.) (2004), *Place and Non-Place: the Reconfiguration of Ireland*, Irish Sociological Chronicles No. 4, Dublin, IPA Press; "Between the mountaintop and the marketplace: New-age travellers, lifestyle politics and the critique of consumer culture" in M. Peillon and E. Slater (eds.) (1998), *Encounters with Modern Ireland*, Irish Sociological Chronicles No. 1, Dublin, IPA Press; "Millenarianism and utopianism in the new Ireland: the tragedy (and comedy) of accelerated modernisation" in C. Coulter and S. Coleman (eds.) (2003), *The End of Irish History?* Manchester: Manchester University Press. These papers have been revised and expanded and are reprinted here with the kind permission of the publishers. Michel Peillon, Mary Corcoran, Colin Coulter, Steve Coleman, Eamon Slater, and others at NUI Maynooth deserve special mention for their ongoing interest and enthusiasm for our work. Thanks to the Department of Sociology at NUI Cork, and to Arpad Szakolczai, whose Research Project on Identity (funded by the Higher Education Authority) supported the hiring of Mervyn Horgan and Derek Chambers as research assistants, who compiled data for the aforementioned chapters under our supervision. Specifically, we would like to thank Brian Keary and the staff at the department of sociology at the University of Limerick, whose support and friendship has been invaluable throughout the duration of this project, and thanks to Pat O'Connor for her strong support of research at UL. Many of these essays were first aired at the Allihies Political Interpretive Sociology workshops; and special thanks to Dave Caffery, graduate students and guests who have participated in these workshops which have been running from 1997. Thanks as well to Brian Langan and to David Givens at The Liffey Press; Brian's incisive editorial comments were invaluable to us in writing up the final draft.

Introduction

"The 'present' denotes the collision of past and future"
(Simmel, 1971: 359).

MUCH PUBLIC DEBATE IN IRELAND today is preoccupied with the rapid rate of social change. Longstanding problems of unemployment and economic underdevelopment are transformed and inverted by newfound affluence and prosperity, yet poverty and social exclusion are rife, and a working couple on average incomes cannot afford a home. Emigration, for one hundred and fifty years a constant and inevitable feature of Irish society, has reversed: emigrants are returning, and immigrants from other societies are arriving, but this migration is unsettling and anxiety-provoking. The Catholic Church, the institutional apparatus that had organised and managed Irish educational and social services, and by virtue of its moral monopoly had governed Irish hearts and minds for at least one hundred years, is in deep crisis: a precipitous decline in vocations, rocked by scandal, its moral authority eclipsed by materialism and consumerism. We celebrate the emergence of our new secular liberal culture, and in the same breath we bemoan the decline of values and the moral bank-ruptcy of modern living. The perennial question of National Unity has been not so much resolved, as subsumed by a peace process that reformulates local conflicts in global con-texts and translates globalised discourses of post-nationalism, multiculturalism and affirmative action into the vernacular of local issues; and yet, historically deep-rooted antagonisms remain as live as ever, irrupting at numerous flashpoints.

We are apt to think that our experience of rapid social change, combined with the persistence and reproduction of old problems in new guises and the uncertainties and ambiva-lence it provokes, is novel and historically recent, but the contemporary experience of accelerated change in Irish soci-ety has resonances and resemblances to earlier periods of dramatic transformation: around the Act of Union in 1800; around the Famine of the 1840s; around the 1920s with In-dependence and the Civil War; the 1960s and early 1970s, with the end of economic protectionism and entry to the EEC. For each period of accelerated change and upheaval, be it the 1800s, 1840s, the 1920s, the 1960s or the 1990s, the *content* is unique and peculiar (the institutions and practices, the cultural phenomena, the events are historically particular) but the *form* (the collective experience of transformation — liminality, disruption, anomie, the feelings of ambivalence pro-voked by change) are common to all.

A brilliant illumination of this recurring pattern in the his-tory of modernisation in Ireland is provided in Angela Bourke's (1999) *The Burning of Bridget Cleary*. In 1895, Michael Cleary, with the help of family and neighbours, burnt his wife Bridget to death. In the subsequent police investigation and trial, which was covered in the international press, it emerged that Bridget Cleary had been delirious with fever, but her husband and others suspected that she had been taken away by the fairies and a "changeling" left in her place. Represented in the press at the time as evidence of Irish rural primitivism, closer examination reveals a more complex reality in which the symbolic orders and imaginative structures of traditional community and modern society co-exist, intermingle, and collide with one another. In the story of the burning of Bridget Cleary, "we witness the collision of town and country, of storytelling and science, of old and new" a reality in which "a modern world of newspapers, courts and railways, and an old world of fairy-belief tradition are brought together with such force that we can still feel the antagonisms and incomprehensions of the 1890s reverberate within our own disputes". [1]

Michael Cleary is both a peasant villager and a modern tradesman, commuting to town for his work as a cooper. Bridget's family live in mud cabins, but she and her husband live in a new model house provided for the respectable working classes by an emerging welfare state. Bridget's domestic life is governed by the morals of traditional patriarchy and the expectation that she bear children, but she has a mind of her own, and her difference, her failure to conform to the *conscience collective* (she is childless, and stylish) is a source of friction with her husband and is taken as a sign of her being bewitched. Michael Cleary had called a doctor, a priest, and a "fairy-man", representatives of three divergent cosmologies, to tend to Bridget.

---

[1] Review comments by Seamus Deane reproduced on the back cover of Bourke (1999).

The tragic story of Bridget Cleary is one of the multiple rationalities that coexist uneasily and often collide with one another in the Irish experience of modernisation and modernity: a story interwoven between the symbolic order and the traditional practices of peasant community and the manifold and various authorities and swarming powers of modern society — the Catholic Church, the police and the legal apparatus of the British empire, modern science, forensics, investigative procedures, rules of evidence, and a modern public — public opinion formed by a national and international mass media. Bridget Cleary (and indeed to an extent some of the other protagonists in the episode) is a prototypical casualty of Ireland's collision culture, crushed between pre-modern and modern social forms, an enchanted world of fairies and *pishogues* and a disenchanted world of medical science and legal-rational authority.

In the contemporary era of globalisation, such cultural clashes or collisions between old and new, global and local, the principles of traditional community and modern society, continue to characterise Irish culture and identity, and indeed have become amplified. Ulrich Beck and Anthony Giddens (1995) have identified an acceleration in the pace of social change through a second-wave, reflexive modernisation. As the generation and dissemination of knowledge in information-rich and communicatively fluent societies increases in intensity and exponentially, due primarily to planetary ecological risk, and growing consciousness of that risk, the speed and degree to which people can grasp and articulate, reflect upon, respond to and act upon change, increases. This acceleration of the process of formation and reformation of consciousness and political and social institutions has unanticipated consequences — including, for example, "traffic jams" and stalemates as the speed of reflexion approaches instantaneity (Virillio 1986), which, in turn, provoke further reflexivity. Thus, Giddens and Beck postulate the arrival of an energised and accelerated, but, as Virilio argues, paradoxically "bogged down", new phase of "reflexive modernisation". Reflexive modernisation generates a paradoxical and ambivalent condition characterised by the simultaneity of acceleration and stasis. Like a car — the quintessential symbol of the ideals of mobility and progress in modernity — on a skidpan: the wheels are spinning but we're going nowhere. Or, at least, in so far as we are accelerating, we have very little control over our direction, and we may be headed for a collision.

Today, Irish social structures and institutions, culture and identity, are being transformed by processes of reflexive — or accelerated — modernisation and globalisation: technologies and markets of production, distribution and consumption generated by transnational corporations; administrative systems, governmental strategies and legal-rational principles developed by post-national and transnational institutions. Globalisation, according to Habermas (2001: 112) is "nothing other than the whirlpool of an accelerating process of modernisation that has been left to its own devices". At the same time, our social structures and institutions are shaped by the re-localisation of the global: local institutions, communitarian norms and principles of action translate and rework exogenous processes of globalisation, attuning them and making them consonant with local institutions. Irish culture and identity is characterised by the ambiguous and paradoxical ways in which the globalisation of the local and the re-localisation of the global are played out, sometimes in concert, sometimes colliding, in a social field crosscut with antagonism.

The local and the global, community and society, tradition and modernity, are not forms of life that supersede one another in linear historical progress, but that exist contemporaneously and interpenetrate with one another, collide and collude with one another, in the time/space of contemporary Ireland. Borders and boundaries between local and global, community and society, tradition and modernity are permeable. We have a foot in both — in many! — camps, and the experience of living in contemporary Ireland is that of living in an in-between world, in-between cultures and identities, an experience of liminality. Ireland is not unique in this experience; we might find similar processes at work, for example, in Spain in the 1980s after Franco's departure, and more recently in the post-communist states of Eastern Europe. Here we are examining the Irish experience in detail, but the concepts we use and the processes we examine may be perhaps generalisable to other experiences outside of Ireland.

The experience of modernisation and modernity in Ireland is ongoing, uneven, and fed by many sources; a multifarious and variegated experience, and hence perhaps best understood with reference to Bauman's (2000) term "liquid modernity". Bauman's metaphor of liquescence captures the notion that there is no such thing as modernity, the modern world, or a singular linear process of modernisation that brought it into being; instead there are multiple modernities, a plurality of "modern worlds", and multiple processes of modernisation.

There are also multiple traditions, for "tradition" refers to a world discursively constructed retrospectively by modernity as a "constitutive outside" from which modernity gains a positive ontology and definition of form. Giddens (1995: 56–7) argues that tradition is a substantive reality *internal* to modernity, an inheritance of pre-modern ideas, institutions and practices that are deeply sedimented and actively reproduced. The retrospective reinterpretation and discursive reconstruction of tradition has been central to the experience of modernisation and modernity. "For most of its history modernity has rebuilt tradition as it has dissolved it . . . the persistence and recreation of tradition has been central to the legitimation of power." Contemporary societies are plural, hybrid, and fluid, and at any one time in modern Ireland there exists a wide variety of times and places and states of consciousness. Sociology must try to co-ordinate and show as equally present a variety of times and places and states of consciousness; for as Simmel says, "the 'present' denotes the collision of past and future. . . . It always contains a bit of the past, and a somewhat smaller bit of the future" (1971: 359).

The studies that follow — of traffic accidents, suicides, celebrity, patterns of consumerism, collective representations, belief and action — are an attempt to explore some of the mélange of modernities and traditions the co-existence and collisions of which animate contemporary Ireland. Our approach is primarily Weberian, in that we seek "interpretively to understand social action and thereby causally to explain it in its course and its effects" (Weber 1978: 4). Here, for example, we understand and interpret traffic collisions in terms of the different rationalities that underpin the action of driving. But as we see it, our discussion of traffic accidents is really a portal, a way into a web of larger questions: namely, an exploration of the Irish experience of modernisation and modernity, and the patterns of social action that show the unique and peculiar ways in which people adapt and cope with accelerated social change.

CHAPTER 1

Road Traffic Accidents and the Experience of Accelerated Modernisation in Ireland[1]

D RIVING IN IRELAND IS A DANGEROUS EXPERIENCE. Those of us who have no choice but to make frequent journeys by road have seen an accident or an accident narrowly averted on almost every trip. Even on trips that pass without incident, there is a "spectre of collision" always there in the form of memorials for the dead at the side of the road and signs of "accident black spots" dotting the main roads. Ireland's road traffic accident rate is double that of the UK, and half that of Portugal, placing it in mid-division in comparative EU terms. Demographic, political-economic and cultural factors influence the rate and pattern of collisions. In Ireland's case, a comparatively young population, which experienced economic boom in the 1990s, means that there is a higher proportion of young inexperienced drivers on the roads. Speeding, principally by young males new to driving, is a factor in most Irish traffic accidents. These demographic and political-economic factors, combined with the role of

---

[1] Co-authored with Mervyn Horgan, York University, Toronto.

alcohol in Irish culture, result in a comparatively high level of accidents (33 per cent) in which alcohol is a factor. The safety of vehicles, attitudes towards the rules of the road and driver behaviour, are also contributory factors.

Ireland's status as a postcolonial, semi-peripheral, dependent society is an important historical and sociological context within which to locate these factors. A general feature of postcolonial cultural legacy can be the state's inability to enforce the law due to an evasive and subversive attitude to rules and regulations and to the law in general. In the realm of material resources, Ireland's comparative economic underdevelopment, with consequently poor infrastructure and dilapidated road system, is a legacy that persisted into the 1970s and 1980s. This period was followed by an economic boom and accelerated modernisation in the 1990s, leading to a rapid increase in the volume of traffic on the roads — doubled between 1990 and 2000 — accelerated growth that outpaces EU-funded infrastructural improvement. In this chapter, we try to draw together and formulate these various factors in terms of a unique and peculiar pattern of Irish road traffic accidents. The general hypothesis investigated below is that road traffic accidents in particular, and Irish society in general, can be understood in terms of collisions, arising from differential paces of life occupying the same time/space.

The new affluence of the "Celtic Tiger" and its associated economic, social and cultural transformations[2] have increased

---

[2] For example, changes in family forms and in rising rates of marital breakdown express a collision between "traditional" versions of masculine and feminine gender roles and "newer" versions of gender facilitated by factors such as lowered fertility, the rapid increase of female labour force participation, and the rise of feminism. See O'Connor, P. (1999).

polarisation between rich and poor, but even for the benefici-
aries of the economic boom, change is experienced as cha-
otic, disruptive. In the words of C. Wright Mills (1959: 4) "the
very shaping of history now outpaces the ability of humans to
orient themselves in accordance with cherished values". The
traffic accident is a spectacular and literal representation of
more general "collisions" occurring in Irish society today: between vestigial traditionalism and accelerated modernisation,
between the local and the global, between the values and organising principles of action of community and society. These
contrasting "worlds" are not distinct polarities or pure forms,
but rather are points on a spectrum which nonetheless pre-
sume a different relationship between the individual and the
collective. For example, on one hand, there is a local driving
culture — a taken-for-granted shared driving practice of local
traffic which prioritises local customs over formal law (for
instance, the right to double-park according to habit and custom) and ascribes to the values of traditional agrarian society
(for instance, in presuming the right of slow-moving farm machinery to delay traffic on a single-lane highway). On the
other hand, there is a commuter driving culture which pre-
sumes a collective commitment to a rational, universalistic,
legal and formal rules of the road, for instance in the unspo-
ken rules that one must always signal, stay in the appropriate
lane, don't block the traffic, drive at the speed limit, and so
on. Coexisting with this is a third culture which is less rational
but more power-driven — i.e. drivers who systematically
break the speed limit, drive in bus lanes, cut across traffic,
etc., and generally act in a selfish, dangerous and illegal manner. This driver is representative of the culture of amplified

individualism, characteristic of modernity, wherein the individual feels free to pursue self-interest over collective norms
and regard for the common good. Inherent in the commuter
driving culture is a commitment to a very particular economy
of time, consistent with Bauman's (1998) description of the
effects of globalisation, whereby members of the first world
are constantly busy and find themselves "short of time", manifest in the lifeworld of driving in the phenomenon of being
nudged over to the shoulder of the road by faster moving
cars, even though one is driving at the speed limit.

The authorities have responded predominantly in two
ways: they have tried, at least to some degree, to "speed up"
local traffic and to "slow down" commuter traffic. Mandatory
NCT testing[3] has been introduced to "rationalise" the local
traffic, to ensure that vehicles are efficient and newer. That
the roadworthiness of a vehicle, according to the National
Roads Authority (1995), is even a contributory factor in less
than one per cent of accidents indicates that the rationale
driving this development is to accelerate the rate of turnover
and consumption, not to protect the environment or to reduce the rate of accidents. There are also concerted campaigns such as "Operation Lifesaver" which involves a sustained media awareness campaign to attune us to the dangers
of speeding; road signs warning that "speed kills", and stating
the numbers of people killed in various regions; signs caution-
ing us to "Slow Down"; an increase in the number of police
speed traps; and other measures. However, as we intend to
demonstrate in this chapter, traffic accidents are not caused

---

[3] The National Car Test, similar to the British MOT test, was introduced
in Ireland in 2000.

by speeding *per se*, or by unsafe vehicles, but rather by the coexistence of two incompatible paces of life on roads only designed to accommodate one pace.

Reducing speeding can to some degree curtail the number of accidents. However, the predominance of single-lane highways in Ireland makes this discrepancy between the pace of even the law-abiding commuter and the local driver deeply problematic. The coexistence causes accidents, yet forcing law-abiding commuters to drive at "local" paces (given the poor state of public transport) would have drastic economic and social ramifications. On the other hand, forcing "locals" to drive at commuter speeds would probably increase the number of accidents. Elsewhere in the EU, roadways are structured to accommodate several paces on dual-lane systems or a choice of roadway versus motorway; this is only done on a piecemeal and inconsistent basis here.

Giddens (1979, 1984) has shown how social life consists of patterns of interaction extending across time and space. This time/space co-ordination of action, the structuration of society, can be thought of in macro terms — the formation of a state and its manifold institutions over a long historical process, for instance — and in terms of how time/space are brought together in the micro processes of the cycles of everyday life. For Giddens, *durée* (time) *locale* (space) and practical consciousness (the tacit knowledgeability of social actors through which they respond to their environment and exercise agency) recursively harmonise with one another in the structuration of normal patterns of social interaction. As we show here, under conditions of accelerated modernisation in contemporary Irish society, we can see the de-structuration of time, space and practical consciousness, and violent collisions that result from interaction not being co-ordinated in space/time.

Commuter traffic, with its emphasis on speed, efficiency, "getting from A to B", illustrates in Weber's (1978, 1958) terms, purposive rational instrumental action, and the tendency of modern life, with its priority of work and time management, to become compartmentalised and divided into segments, whereby work is separated from leisure, private from public, the corporate from the personal. Local traffic, which prioritises "stopping for a chat", "picking up a few groceries", "dropping off the kids", and the numerous and various car-based social interactions that comprise the substantive rationality anchoring family and community living, integrates these disparate spheres, and as such resists this compartmentalisation. But driving practices grounded in substantive rationality coexist with the pace of commuter traffic and shares the same roadways, illustrating the spatial/temporal and the moral-practical disunity of contemporary Irish life. People are faced with the complex and stressful task of reconciling these two realms and contradictory rationalities in the artful practice of everyday life. Drivers are frequently both commuters at certain times and locals at others, as we occupy numerous overlapping subject positions. When parents drop their kids off to the crèche or school on the way to work they must simultaneously orient themselves with instrumental rationality to rush-hour traffic, and at the same time be attuned with affective rationality to their child in the back seat.

Furthermore, a considerable portion of driving can be understood in terms of Weber's (1978) category of traditional action. For example, many of the patterns of action that drivers rely on for the successful performance of the routine and mundane everyday practices of driving, including such actions as steering, braking, changing gears, the use of pedals, instruments, the controls of their vehicle, and such habits (good or bad) that they have picked up, developed, and routinised, such as checking rear-view mirrors or riding the clutch, are unreflexive, automatic, or mechanical forms of action: actions we perform without thinking. Accidents at new junctions and roundabouts illustrate the role of traditional action in driving, as such accidents are typically caused by regular users who "know" the road and who "forget about" or "don't see" the changed layout and drive on as they have been accustomed to doing.[4]

According to Giddens (1991) a defining characteristic of modernity is that the harmonisation of action in time/space is premised on actors' trust in "expert systems", abstract, "disembedded" systems of "technical accomplishment and professional expertise that organise large areas of the material and social environments in which we live" (ibid.: 27).

> When I go out of the house and get into a car, I enter settings that are thoroughly permeated by expert knowledge — involving the design and construction of automobiles, highways, intersections, traffic lights, and many other items. . . . I have minimal knowledge about the technicalities and modes of road building, the maintaining of road surfaces, or the computers which help control the movement of traffic. . . . Everyone

---

[4] See, for example, Tim Phillips and Philip Smith (2000), "Police violence occasioning citizen complaint: an empirical analysis of time-space dynamics", *British Journal of Criminology*, 40, 480–496.

> knows that driving a car is a dangerous activity, entailing
> the risk of accident. In choosing to go out in the car, I
> accept that risk, but rely on the aforesaid expertise to
> guarantee that it is minimised as far as possible.
> (Giddens, 1991: 28)

Modern expert systems coexist and intermingle with traditional systems of rules and practices that are embedded, ha-
bitual, and organised on different principles. Expert systems
can overlap these systems, but they can also be discontinuous with them, and collide with them. Under conditions of
accelerated modernisation in Ireland, the disjunctions between disembedded and embedded systems of rationality
are exacerbated, and the risk of accidents increases.

A Unique and Particular Pattern of Irish Road Traffic Accidents[5]

Our empirical investigations include examination of accident
statistics and periodic Reports of the National Roads Authority, which covers all of the Republic of Ireland. While NRA
statistics provide an overview of accident rates, fatalities and
injuries by age and gender, rates on national primary and
other routes, rates by urban/rural, day/night, as well as contributory factors such as alcohol and seat-belt use, NRA statistics are not compiled in such a way as to facilitate a more
detailed sociological study of accident patterns. Thus, the
NRA overview of accident rates is explored in greater depth
through a body of evidence provided by key informant
interviews with senior Gardaí working with the traffic corps
of several divisions, covering both urban and rural areas.

---

[5] Details of accidents have been altered to ensure anonymity.

Traffic corps Gardaí in fact compile the accident reports from which the NRA statistics are abstracted. In the process of NRA statistics gathering, the content of the Garda accident reports with the telling sociological details are omitted. Here we return to the source of this information, to the traffic corps Gardaí themselves, to compile our empirical data. These traffic corps Gardaí identified accident "black-spots" in their jurisdictions, and they could readily characterise a typical pattern of accidents at these locations. In addition, we interviewed senior engineers with responsibility for road construction and maintenance in several local authority areas, including the cities and counties of Dublin, Cork, Limerick, Galway, and Louth. These include the main urban centres, their commuter-belts, the inter-city national primary (NP) roads that link them, and their rural hinterlands. Like the traffic corps Gardaí, the local authority road engineers were able to identify hazardous roads and typical accident patterns, and these corroborated the accounts of traffic corps Gardaí. The data provided by these empirical investigations reveal a number of distinct types of accidents, forming the pattern of collision culture outlined in the introduction, wherein road traffic accidents are symptomatic of the coexistence of incommensurable forms of life in the same space/time.

The National Roads Authority (1994) identifies the pattern of road traffic collisions in contemporary Ireland as follows:

> The accident rate is influenced by, *inter alia*, the quality of the road. For example, the personal injury accident rate on the three routes N7 Dublin to Limerick, N11 Dublin to Rosslare and N6 Kinnegad to Galway which

> are already half completed to international standards is
> 30 per cent below the average for the National Primary
> network. In contrast, the accident rate on the NI
> Dublin to Belfast which is only 20 per cent completed
> to the required standard is 30 per cent above average.
>
> It is clear that the accident rate is lowest on those
> roads that have been improved to international
> standard. It can be expected that the accident rate will
> decline as the Authority's programme for improving
> the national road network is fully implemented.

The Irish for "road" is *bóthar*, which translates literally as *bó*
(cow) *thar*, from the verb *tar/thar*, to pass, to come over, to
come across (Dineen: 1927). *Bóthar* means "the cow's passage". As the cow wanders along, following the contour of
the land, over time it wears a track on the earth. This is the
road corresponding to, and formed by, a traditional form of
life. Secondary meanings of *bóthar* are "habits, schemes, ways
of doing things". By contrast, the modernist architect Le
Corbusier (1924) calls a motorway "a machine for traffic"; it
is planned, engineered on principles of instrumental rationality, to link two points as quickly and efficiently as possible.
Natural "obstacles" are bulldozed, blasted, bridged, and
bored through. Le Corbusier proclaims: "A crooked road is
a donkey's track. A straight road is a path for man." The uneven and discontinuous pattern of modernisation in Ireland
has resulted in what the Irish Automobile Association describes as "a patchwork quilt that alternates between highways and traditional bottlenecks".[6]

---

[6] C. Faughnan, Irish Automobile Association, quoted in B. Lavery (2000),
"Safety messages getting through to Irish drivers", *New York Times*, 27
October.

According to traffic corps Gardaí, a very common type of collision occurs at the intersection where the *bóthar* meets the motorway. This occurs where an intercity, national primary (NP) road is intersected by a minor road, for example, at Daly's Cross on the Limerick–Dublin road, (N7) or at Rourke's Cross on the Limerick–Cork route (N20), where a fast, straight stretch of NP road is intersected by a minor road from Kilmallock and Newcastlewest (R518) at a local shop/filling station. At such junctions, intercity traffic meets rural traffic. The "R" in "R518" designates "Regional", and the intersection, the crossroads named as "Daly's", or "Rourke's", a nomenclature common throughout rural Ireland, signifies that this is where the Dalys, the Rourkes, or some other family, have lived for generations.

The general pattern at such intersections is illustrated by particular examples from the National Roads Authority data bank: a customer pulling out from the local shop/filling station is struck by a light goods vehicle travelling from Limerick to Dublin; a car and trailer turning right from the N20 to the R518 is rear-ended by a car ongoing to Limerick; a 65-year-old man, driving a fourteen-year-old car, on the way to mass, is involved in a fatal collision with an intercity driver in a new Range Rover. The case of the hazardous intersection at Rourke's Cross is especially over-determined with significance, as the R518 is the road to Bruree, birthplace of Eamon de Valera, the father of Irish independence and architect of the economic and cultural development strategy of self-sufficiency that framed the development of Irish society for most of the twentieth century. De Valera infamously articulated a communitarian vision of Ireland as "a parish writ large"; a modern society, but anchored by rural, Catholic, traditional values, in which athletic youths and comely maidens from cosy homesteads gathered at the crossroads to dance.[7] It is precisely at that crossroads where de Valera's Ireland meets the accelerated modernisation of the Celtic Tiger that collisions occur.

An inverse variation on this theme is illustrated by a tragic accident in which a retired couple were killed in a collision in the midlands. A car struck them as they were walking along a national primary road. The pair had recently moved from America to live in the Irish countryside. Within their frame of reference, the road on which they were walking was not a motorway like those they had left behind in Philadelphia. They were strolling abreast along an Irish boreen.[8] Their world collided with that of a young man — their neighbour, the son of a local farmer — for whom this was no longer a country road where one might be likely to meet people out walking, but the main road to Dublin where he was rushing to work. And, in this example, we can also see one of the characteristic inversions of the economy of desire animating the process of globalisation: the American couple — they might as easily have been German, French, or British — move to Ireland, which they imagine as marginal, a place apart, offering respite from hyper-rationalisation and urban congestion, the pathologies of over-development, only to collide with the Irish rushing to pursue the fantasy of progress and prosperity through

---

[7] M. Moyinhan (ed.) (1980), *Speeches and Statements of Eamon de Valera: 1917–1973*, Dublin: Gill & Macmillan.

[8] *Boreen*, a colloquial abbreviation of *bothair-ín*, translates as "a little cow's track", i.e. a small road.

rationalisation and urbanism, which they imagine the Americans and the Germans have already realised.

Similar situations exist throughout the Irish roads network. Traffic corps Gardaí, for example, identify as hazardous the numerous instances where a NP route passes through villages, posing a danger to pedestrians, cyclists and children — the typical traffic of village life. The hazard is exacerbated in that delays are common at these bottlenecks,, leading to increased frustration and aggressive driving afterwards. Examples identified by Gardaí include the villages of Birdhill (Dublin–Limerick N7) Crusheen (Limerick–Galway N18) Halfway and Buttevant (Limerick–Cork N20) Rathcormack (Dublin–Cork N8), and countless others. A typical case is that of an accident on the N2, which carries heavy traffic from Northern Ireland to Dublin: a juggernaut failed to negotiate an ancient bridge on a bend in the centre of a village and collided with two cars, killing three people. The responses to this typical pattern of collisions vary. In extreme cases where there are long delays and a high number of fatalities, bypasses may be constructed, as in the cases of Athlone (Dublin–Galway N6), Croom (Cork–Limerick N20), Newmarket-on-Fergus (Limerick–Galway N18), Portlaoise (Limerick–Dublin N7), and several others. The more usual response involves a combination of low-cost engineering measures (road markings, signs, lighting) and increased Garda speed checks. Such "traffic calming" strategies seek to decelerate the speed of modernisation to be compatible with the pace of rural, village, local life, are usually marked by road signs reading: "Caution: Slow Through Village", or "Caution: Experimental Traffic Calming Measures Ahead".

Another type of collision belonging to the same pattern of incompatible paces of life occupying the same space/time, occurs on stretches of NP roads that have already been improved to international standards, according to the terms of the NRA — and indeed this type of accident to some extent confounds the relationship between improved roads and reduced accidents outlined in the NRA Report. In these cases, the NP carriageway is improved — straightened, widened, cambered, surfaced, lined — and sometimes villages are bypassed. Yet some of these improved stretches continue to have high numbers of accidents; for example, the Rathkeale bypass, on the national primary route between Limerick and Killarney (N21) and on the Cork–Mallow new road (N20). The reason why there continues to be a high rate of collisions on these improved roads is that intercity traffic shares space with local and rural traffic, turning on and off the main route to surrounding parishes and villages. For example, the new Cork–Mallow road is 19 miles long, making Mallow a commuter town for Cork city. The new road, which carries intercity as well as commuter traffic, is intersected by 26 minor roads, not counting innumerable entrances/exits to farms and houses. At these minor intersections, there are no underpasses or flyovers, which would enable traffic to enter and exit the main stream of traffic without interruption.

Therefore, a typical collision identified by Gardaí occurs when a vehicle is joining the main road from a minor road, or turning right off the main road to join a minor road. The vehicle must come to a halt in the centre of the roadway and cross against oncoming traffic. Frequently, collisions involve the stationary vehicle being rear-ended by an ongoing vehicle that encounters it in what would ordinarily be the fast lane. The Accident and Emergency Consultant Surgeon at a major Irish teaching hospital identifies this type of collision as the most common cause of road deaths and serious injuries seen by his department. Death and serious injury could be very significantly reduced, he says, by the construction of motor-way-style exits (exiting to the left and traversing by flyover) at such intersections.[9] This problem even occurs on Ireland's dual carriageways, of which there are very few: 90 per cent of the road network, including improved roads, remains single-lane. On the dual carriageway between Limerick and Shannon Airport — which carries intercity traffic, commuter traffic, local traffic, as well as being a major tourist point of entry — in one mile of roadway there are four hazardous intersections: two junctures at which stationary traffic merges with the fast lane; another where traffic exits from the fast lane; and another, where traffic from a minor intersection must cross at right angles to two lanes of traffic from the right, wait in the middle of the carriageway, and then merge with the fast lane of traffic coming from the left. [10]

A common variation on this theme is when a national primary route is intersected by "cows crossing", where herds of cattle cross at milking time from pasture to parlour. Again, throughout the national roads network, such instances are

---

[9] Dr Tony Martin, consultant surgeon, A&E, University College Hospital Galway, interviewed for this paper on 19 December 2001.

[10] Improvements to the road, completed in 2004, have solved these long-standing problems. However, the danger is now moved five miles further down the road towards Ennis, where the improved dual carriageway abruptly ends at the Dromoland interchange, immediately before a narrow bridge.

literally countless. On the N20, for example, between Charleville and Buttevant, a distance of less than 10 miles, there are 16 "cows crossing" junctures. A further variation is "farm machinery crossing", signifying the hazard of tractors and agricultural machinery emerging from gateways or moving slowly along major roads. Farmers delivering bales and winter fodder are a particular hazard, as frequently their machinery is inadequately lit or its lights are obscured by the load or by dirt. As well as the farmer on an old tractor with poor lights, this is also the traffic of modern industrial-scale agriculture: silage and harvesting contractors who work at high intensity, working late into the night, and who move machinery from job to job on NP roads. Such slow-moving traffic causes tailbacks and occasions driver frustration and dangerous overtaking. On the N20, a car overtaking a slow-moving vehicle towing a cattle trailer collided with an oncoming car, killing four.

An inverse variation of this pattern occurs when commuter traffic seeks to avoid the rush-hour traffic on NP roads by taking short cuts and alternative routes through minor rural roads. Now, slow-moving local traffic and agricultural vehicles find themselves forced to accommodate high-speed through traffic on roads which they had previously been accustomed to regarding as "theirs". Galway, the fastest-growing city in Europe, is a notable example: as its network of new highways and ring-roads have already become congested, commuters have appropriated older backroads and by-ways through surrounding rural communities as access routes to and from the city.[11]

---

[11] "Backroad city traffic posing a new danger", *Galway City Tribune*, 23 June 2000, p. 5.

A further nuance on this theme are what Garda informants called "freak" accidents, such as one in which a concrete block fell from a truck and smashed through the windscreen of a car travelling behind, killing the driver. Similar accidents, Gardaí say, have been caused by dirt, effluent, or mud on the road near a building site or farm activity, leading to dirty windscreens and reduced visibility, as well as stones, building materials, wrapping from silage bales strewn on the roadway. To call these "freak" accidents is a misnomer, as they are better interpreted in terms of collision culture: accidents resulting from the debris of tradition and the excess of modernisation.

A case study that illustrates all of the above themes in the pattern of road traffic accidents of collision culture is the case of Louth. Louth lies between Dublin and Northern Ireland. The N1, the national primary route between Dublin and Belfast, transects the entire region. The N2, N3 and N4, and a considerable portion of Dublin's airport and seaport traffic also pass through the region. Drogheda, Dundalk and several small county towns fall within what has become the "greater Dublin area" commuter belt, while at the same time much of the region comprises rural hinterland. This region has the highest road traffic accident rate in the country, 30 per cent higher than average, so much so that car-owners in the Louth Local Authority region pay substantially higher insurance premiums than anywhere else in Ireland. The vast majority of traffic accidents in Louth between 1991 and 1995 are clustered at intersections where national primary routes are intersected by minor roads.

A particularly high number of accidents occur at the first junction at the southern side of the border with Northern Ireland, immediately after motorists leave the motorway system in Northern Ireland and encounter the Republic's national primary route network. Interestingly, where a major road improvement has been made in Louth — a new, faster, motorway has replaced the N1 — there have been only two accidents, the lowest on any comparable stretch of national primary roadways in the region. The accident rate increases again at the points north and south, where the improved roadway ends. At one of these junctures, described in the local press as a "zone of conflict", five or six hundred cars per day cross the new motorway while 8,000 vehicles pass through.[12] Two incidents from this case study illustrate the general hypothesis of collision culture. The first is a fatal accident that occurred on the new highway only three days after the Minister for the Environment had officiated at the opening ceremony, when an elderly man cycling on the motorway was in a fatal collision with a car.[13] The second relates to the discussions of the Local Authority Council in relation to the dangers of the new motorway. One Councillor reported that many local people, including himself, felt that the new road was dangerous, and had decided not to use it at all, reflecting a more generalised anxiety about the hazards of accelerated modernisation. Another Councillor

---

[12] "Just three days after opening of motorway elderly man is killed", *The Argus*, 22 October 1993, p. 27.

[13] Ibid.

remarked that "whatever about cars, it was virtually impossible to cross the new motorway by tractor".[14]

This phenomenon, where an accident black spot coincides with the point where an improved roadway ends — where the motorway reverts to the *bother* — is repeated throughout the country's road network, and again is richly symptomatic of the fundamental problem underpinning the phenomenon of collision culture: the uneasy co-existence of incongruous and often incompatible forms and paces of life in the same time/space. On the N21 between Killarney and Limerick, there is a large sign stating: "This Project [road construction] is 80% Financed by the European Structural Fund". The following stretch of the N21 is of similar quality to a German autobahn. Then, as the road crests a hill and descends towards the town of Newcastlewest, a sign abruptly states: "Caution: Improved Roadway Ends Now", followed, 100 metres later, by an "accident black spot".

Becoming an Experienced Irish Driver: Reflexivity, Adaptation, and the Reconciliation of Divergent Social Logics

Irish driving culture can be understood and interpreted as an idiomatically unique and peculiar way in which members of a society living through collision culture make their world meaningful, and generate and institutionalise principles of action, value orientations and normative standards appropriate to their situation. As Weber (1978) points out, actions are never "rational" or "irrational" in the abstract, as though

---

[14] "Splendid new motorway must not become just another deadly speed track", in ibid.

they can be judged from some Archimedean point outside of their social context. Rather, there are multiple forms of rationality, which, from the point of view of actors, are valid and meaningful within the historically situated web of social signification in which they are suspended, and which they themselves have woven (Geertz, 1993). In this spirit de Certeau (1984) enables us to collect the various specific and peculiar idiomatic phenomena of Irish driving culture in terms of the artful tactics that are woven into the practice of everyday life, that show, as Simmel (1971b) says, the meaningful ways in which members reconcile the divergent trajectories of life's inner processes.

Collision culture, the flux and reflux, decomposition and recomposition, of the contents and forms of life in contemporary Ireland, has a three-fold structure: *collision* — the encounter of incommensurate forms of life in the same time/space; *trauma* — the social ruptures arising from such collisions, exemplified here by the road traffic accident; and third, *recuperation* — the stage of recovery, rebuilding, whereby people try to make sense of the collision, cope with the damage, restore social order, learn to carry on with life and make the best of the changed situation. Collision culture is structured in the same way as the rite of passage is structured, according to Turner's (1967, 1985) celebrated anthropological analysis: the prior existing social order, which is breached and dissolved, followed by a period of crisis or liminality, during which a previous identity dies, is sloughed off and discarded, followed by a stage of reintegration and reconstruction in which social order is restored and a new identity is assumed. Building on Turner's work, Szakolczai

(2000) further unpacks the relationship between identity formation and liminal experiences, showing how "ex-per-ience" means "to live through" — itself a tri-phase structure, the middle term "per", from Sanskrit, meaning "danger", as in "peril", for example. In this instance, we have the individual and collective experience of social transformation in con-temporary Irish society, marked by peoples' individual and collective living through the collisions of elements of tradi-tional and modern forms of life — a dangerous, perilous ex-perience, exemplified by the car crash; and following this cri-sis, we can find recuperation, the constitution of a new iden-tity, reintegration, and the restoration of social order.

The rapid pace of social transformation in Ireland today generates liminality and anomie, and this is the background against which road traffic collisions can be interpreted. A florid symptom of the social pathology of anomie and how it relates to road traffic is provided in the proliferation of road-signs that caution Irish drivers to take care as driving condi-tions are risky, changing and uncertain. These cautionary road signs include such examples as: "Welcome to Galway", followed 100 metres later by "In the Last 4 Years 141 People Have Been Killed on Roads in Co. Galway"; "Speed Kills"; "Slow Down"; "Caution Road Works Ahead"; "Caution Slip-pery Surface"; "Caution Uneven Surface"; "Caution Changed Layout Ahead"; "Caution No Road Markings"; "Caution Ex-perimental Traffic Calming Ahead"; "Caution Improved Road Ends Now"; "Caution You Are Now Entering a High Acci-dent Area"; "Caution Oncoming Traffic May be in Middle of the Road"; and "Wise Up, Slow Down, Expect the Unex-pected". Wittgenstein says that "to imagine a language is to imagine a form of life" (1994: 8). What form of life does the language of Irish road signs intimate? Let us first take the signs at face value: the signs mean what they say. They directly signify the reality of Irish road conditions, and insofar as Irish road conditions are ambiguous, the signs signify liminality and anomie, the broader currents of collision culture.

Signs also signify the "Rules of the Road". They signify a formal grammar, a moral code, a system of rules that can be learned and obeyed. The road signs intimate and imagine an ideal form of driving (driving by the rules) and posit an imagined ideal type driver (who knows and obeys the rules) against which actual driving practice is reflexively formed. In other words, with reference to the ideal form of driving imagined in the rules of the road and institutionalised in the law, within the terms of this model the real practices of the normal driver (the normative practice of driving) becomes established by drivers self-reflexively reforming their driving practices to conform to the law and to live up to the ideal. The law is itself changed and re-formed over time by this process of reflexivity. The ideal intimated by the formal grammar of the rules of the road constitutes a regulative standard, a limit horizon, which makes possible the institutionalisation of normal — that is to say, formal — good driving. This cognitive learning process is what is presupposed in the theory and practice divisions in the driving licence examination: has the driver learned the rules, and does his/her driving practice conform to the rules? This cognitive internalisation of the ideal intimated by the rules of the road as a matter of individual and collective learning is an aspect of the formation of good driving. However, it is not the same thing as good driving formed by living through the experience of collision culture, as any driving instructor knows, and as an ethnomethodology of good driving practices (the normative content of the driving practices of experienced Irish drivers) reveals.

Durkheim stresses the need for moral order as response to anomie generated by transition between different forms of society. Simmel emphasises instead that we try to see how new emerging social forms collect the tensions of conflicting desires that are constitutive of life's inner processes. The task is "neither to condone or to complain [i.e. to be affirmative or critical] but to understand" (1971a: 339); in this case, to understand how the forms and types of Irish society give expression to the reconciliation of tensions that are unique and peculiar to Irish life. In this case, we want to show how becoming an experienced driver in Ireland, and the normative practices — that is, the good driving — of experienced Irish drivers, illustrates the ways in and through which members living through collision culture artfully improvise and institutionalise ways to cope with anomic driving conditions (itself symptomatic of anomie in the broader society) and reconstitute social order.

The commonsense misunderstanding that accidents are caused by speeding, or that "driver error" is responsible for 80 per cent of accidents on Irish roads, is grievously misleading. First, it simply reflects the exaggeration of the individual as the morally responsible agent and the locus of blame, a peculiar conceit of modernity. Second, the emphasis on driver error misses the point, and obscures the extent to which driving, for the most part, is an artful accomplishment in which drivers exemplify great skill and resourcefulness. In the context of dangerously anomic driving conditions, good driving in Ireland is an art of interpretation, improvisation, making do. In de Certeau's terms in *The Practice of Everyday Life*, Irish drivers are *bricoleurs* — "handy-men". Under liminal conditions, where there are "no road markings ahead" and "changed layouts" we are thrown into the position of having to become "handymen". The handiwork in question, de Certeau says, is artful and inventive — "crafty" in the sense of a skilled and imaginative use of materials that are at hand. We invent tactics to help us to cope with the changed situation; we make do, we improvise. However, "invention is not unlimited, and like improvisations on the piano or on the guitar, it presupposes the knowledge and application of codes . . . and implies a logic of the operation of actions relative to types of situations" (de Certeau, 1984: 21). To reconstitute social order under anomic conditions of social transformation, that is, in the micro-sociological context considered here, to come up with new rules of the road, normative driving standards to govern good practice amongst Irish road users, drivers must already have a *habitus* (a repertoire of lived experience) including driving habits built up, and often incorporated as bodily *hexis* (a body of experience) which they can draw from to improvise.

The experienced driver has already in a sense learned to live through and survive dangerous driving conditions. Most experienced drivers will articulate their experience in terms of having been in an accident themselves, or having had some "close shaves" over the years, or having had someone close to them killed or injured. To "survive" bears what Wittgenstein (1958) would call a strong family resemblance to experience, in that "sur-vive" (the French *sur* from Latin *super* meaning beyond, above, and *vivre*, to live, to exist, to be) means to continue to live/exist, especially after coming close to dying or being destroyed or being in a difficult or threatening situation. To survive is to endure: to have lived through and transcended the peril to life.[15] The identity of the survivor is transformed: the experienced driver is a different form of life. Experienced drivers will "know" and anticipate dangerous bends and junctions, places and situations that they "have learned from experience" to "watch out for"; places where someone "is going to get caught" [be in a collision] overtaking, pulling out, turning off. Experience is the aggregate effect, the fusion over time, of living through and having survived traumatic incident(s) and sustained exposure to the danger and knowledge of the risk of trauma.

The cultural specificity of becoming an experienced driver means that driving experience does not necessarily travel between different cultural contexts. North American and continental tourists may well be experienced drivers, but they may not have experience of vehicles with right-hand drive or manual transmission, and they may be more familiar with highway, urban and motorway driving, all conditions that are quite different on Irish roads. Visitors and tourists, therefore, may find driving in Ireland hazardous, or indeed their driving may be hazardous to other drivers on Irish roads. That being an experienced driver is not the same thing as being an experienced *Irish* driver is illustrated by the case of an English tourist with over twenty years' experience as a

---

[15] From the *Oxford English Dictionary* and the *Cambridge International Dictionary*.

professional lorry driver in the UK and Europe. There, the equivalent of Ireland's national primary routes would typically be motorways and dual carriageways from which slow-moving machinery would often be segregated or prohibited. He was killed while on a motoring holiday in Ireland when his car collided with an agricultural vehicle at a farm entrance on the N72. It is in this context that we might locate the specific problem of the young and inexperienced driver. Like the tourist, and unlike the *bricoleur*, he has nothing to build on.

We will return to the inexperienced driver again, but first let us examine the tricks of the trade, the artful practices, the survival tactics of Irish drivers as they learn to cope with the experience of collision culture. Irish drivers habitually and fluently communicate with other drivers: they salute, gesture, they comment on dangerous situations and on others' driving by facial expressions. In rural contexts they hail each other with a local dialect of nods and winks: in west Cork, a nod, in east Clare, an index finger of the right hand raised off the steering wheel as drivers pass each other or pass neighbours walking. This is a traditional "ideological hailing" in the Althusserian (1984) sense: it interpellates members of a shared world — "Hey, you there", "I know you, you know me, we're members of this community". It also interpellates the stranger to account for himself. When a local hails a stranger — which they do, all the time, and which tourists in the Irish countryside misrecognise as "the friendly locals" — they are asking, "Who's that fellow there? Do we know him? Is he one of us?" They are saying, "Hey, you there"; "We see you"; "We're watching you". By such a language, local communities constitute themselves, maintain their boundaries, and protect themselves. For experienced Irish drivers, these communicative actions are part of habitus and even bodily hexis anchored in traditional forms of life. They are sedimented, automatic, unreflexive, and vestigial (exemplified in the phenomenon, common even amongst young Irish drivers, of making the sign of the cross as they pass churches, cemeteries and grottoes) but they form a vital part of the rich reservoir and repertoire that Irish driving draws from and improvises with.

This habitus extends to the materiality of experienced drivers' cars. Such drivers say how they "know" their cars: it is familiar and "second nature" for them; they use their vehicles as prosthetic extensions of their communicative bodies to speak with one another. For example, the driver of a faster-moving vehicle may flash headlights at the driver in front, requesting room to overtake. Once, from a distance that is close but is not tailgating, is normal. More than once, or tailgating too closely, is seen as aggressive — "Get out of my way". An experienced driver of a slower-moving vehicle will usually not have to be "asked", but will move over automatically, as a matter of courtesy. When the driver has overtaken, it is customary that the other's good practice be acknowledged. Drivers do this by briefly turning on their hazard lights. Their "Thank yous" are in turn acknowledged by the driver of the vehicle that has been overtaken flashing his headlights, "You're welcome".

These practices, seemingly insignificant, are of fundamental importance. They constitute the elementary practices of an emerging social form, developed from traditional action combined with instrumental and strategic rationality, to improvise a substantively rational, normative action appropriate to the situation, wherein members acknowledge the plurality of road usage, the anomic context that all members share, and their mutual commitment to negotiating and reconstituting a normative order that can accommodate them. As well, the communicative actions of drivers who use their vehicles as bodily prostheses subverts and resists the hyper-rationalisation and depersonalisation of the highway as a "machine for traffic" and reinscribes on it a human language. To participate in this civic work of structuration, reconstituting social order, is to show good form. To violate the emerging convention shows bad form, and incurs annoyance and sanctions: drivers sometimes respond to rude overtakers by not only not pulling over, but by moving out and slowing down, as though to say "I'll teach you some manners". On a particularly bad stretch of the N6 where a number of pedestrians have been killed by weekend traffic passing through from Dublin to Galway, the local community has placed white crosses reminiscent of those on a battlefield along the roadside and, reportedly, have adopted the practice of driving at no more than 50 mph close to the centre of the road, making it virtually impossible for fast-moving through-traffic to overtake or to speed through their community.

Traffic corps Gardaí readily informed us that good driving practices are a matter of "road manners", "courtesy", and "driver etiquette"; that is, norms of good driving governing collective behaviour of road use. This is true of drivers everywhere, not just in Ireland. Elias (1995) argues that the long-run downward trend in car accident fatalities in western societies is a result of the "civilising process". Much normal driving depends upon shared taken-for-granted informal codes of practice, institutionalised and subjectively internalised "good road manners" — for example, pulling over to let faster traffic overtake, letting people merge, giving right of way on narrow streets — as much as it depends on knowledge and practice of the formal rules of the road. The social form is general — experienced English, German or American drivers no doubt have developed their own codes of good practice — but the *content* of road manners may be culturally specific and locally particular. Road anomie emerges as conditions change and different behaviours compete with different norms that are operative simultaneously. Experienced drivers respond to the new experience by developing new codes of practice, built on and out of existing practices.

Frequently, Gardaí say, the new codes "are not legal, strictly speaking, but they work well enough". Some examples of these tricks, provided by Gardaí, include a practice that has developed on a stretch of the N17 intersected by numerous minor roads, where there have been several fatalities: "When a vehicle is going to turn right off the major road to a minor road, rather than simply indicating, the driver turns on hazard flashers, often as much as a mile before he's going to turn off. This gets the attention of the driver coming up behind, who might be just focused on getting from A to B." Another traffic corps Garda told us of a practice that has developed at a conjuncture on the N21: local traffic drive contra-flow on the hard shoulder for short distances between two minor intersections, which, though he says "sounds like madness, is probably safer than having to cross twice". Against that, and to underline the dangerous ambiguity, the same Garda went on to say how the hard shoulder on many roads is used in practice as a slow lane, so that drivers informally transform certain stretches of single lane roads into dual carriageways. Another Garda explained an informal practice that has developed at a busy roundabout where traffic from a new industrial estate, passing through suburban housing estates, joins a national primary route. The rule is, of course, "yield right of way" but the traffic flow from the right is so heavy that if the rule were obeyed, traffic from the estate would never get out. For a time, Gardaí did point duty at the roundabout at busy periods, but after a short while they found that it was unnecessary, as drivers using the intersection developed their own code of practice, letting every second car take its turn. "Not legal at all, but it works as well, or better, than anything we could do", said the Garda. "As a matter of fact," he went on, "we ended up watching out for the fellows that didn't play the game, that wouldn't give people their turn", i.e. the driver who stuck to the letter of the law, rather than adapted to the spirit of the usage of the new rule being formed.

This is illustrative of the fact that policemen are members too. Like civilians living through the experience of collision culture, they do not simply enforce the law, but to some extent, within the range of discretionary power at their disposal, they interpret, improvise, and adapt bureaucratic legal rationality to suit the anomic context of the wider society. Again, it is the experienced Garda, drawing from a habitus wherein bureaucratic legal and substantive affective rationalities overlap, who is able to make judgements based on experience that are suited to the liminal contexts of collision culture. One such Garda explained that, even though the speed limit is 60 mph, "there are stretches of main roads where even 40 miles an hour is dangerous, and others where, in fairness, 75 miles an hour wouldn't be unreasonable. On a good stretch of road, if someone were going along at 65, or 68 even, we'd hardly pull him for that. The important thing there is that he sees us and goes a bit easier. But the fellow really going hard, now we'll pull him for sure."

Conclusion

The uneven process of development in contemporary Ireland is reflected in the traumatic phenomenon of road traffic accidents. The newfound affluence and the decline of a traditional moral hegemony have presented young Irish people with tremendous new freedoms and opportunities. Young people are no longer forced to emigrate; they have work, opportunities, and money to spend. They have choices to make, things to do and places to go. Perhaps — and this is the paradox and the tragedy — too much so: infinite choices, limitless horizons, insatiable desires, a condition of morbidity and danger. Speed (in a context of limitlessness a speed limit becomes a meaningless anachronism), recklessness (for there is confusion as to the moral authority to reckon with), and the egoistic sense that one "owns the road", are the equivalent subjective manifestations of anomie and egoism amongst the young inexperienced male drivers who are involved in over half of all accidents. This is the source of the particular danger that they represent to themselves and other road users in contemporary Ireland.

While speeding is often a factor in road traffic accidents, the more specific problem in Irish accidents is the coexistence of two paces of traffic on highways only designed to hold one. Thus the state's anti-speeding campaign and the "penalty points" system, however effective they are in the short term, deflect attention from the importance of developing strategies that will allow for a diversity of paces of life and of traffic which coexist in Ireland, such as continuous two-lane highways and better and more efficient, publicly owned inter-city mass transit, strategies which would have a much more profound and lasting effect in reducing fatalities but which would be expensive. It remains to be seen how the broader collisions underlying our analysis can become alleviated. In the meantime, we have shown that in the liminal spaces between traditional and modern forms of life, Irish people artfully and heroically invent ways of coping and facing the future.

CHAPTER 2

Unanticipated Consequences of Accelerated Modernisation: The Sheedy Case

IN THE 1960S, ON THE ROAD between the towns of Bantry and Glengarriff in west Cork, two cars were in a minor collision. No one was injured, fortunately, and the two drivers got out of their cars and began to remonstrate with one another. These were no ordinary motorists, as at that time and place to possess a car belonged to a symbolic order and a chain of equivalences that was synonymous with status and power. One of the drivers was the retired Chief Surgeon of the Royal Navy, who was living in the area, and the other was the Catholic Parish Priest of Bantry. Both men sought to define the situation in his own favour. Tempers were frayed and voices were raised. "Look here!" said the naval officer, "Do you have any idea to whom you are speaking?" "Faith, no then, I do not", said the PP. "I am," announced the former, giving his full title, "Sir Arthur, Doctor Stanley Nance". "Arrah . . ." says the other, "Sir Arthur eejit!"

This story is part of local lore around Bantry. An uncle of one of the authors told it in the pub, and the company laughed heartily. It is a story of powers colliding; the vestiges of the British Empire clash with the Irish Catholic Church at it zenith. The parish priest, representative of the hegemony of de Valera's Catholic peasant Republic, collides with the remnant of the former power who sought to assert his rank by invoking the register and discourse of the empire, and the priest curtly, confidently, dismisses him in the local vernacular, the idiom of the reigning power. The parish priest is at one with the common people and with the official ideology of de Valera's Republic. This constitutes the hegemony of traditionalism in twentieth-century Ireland. A collective conscience is coextensive with the social body, pervading the institutions of church, state and community, and despite the enormous differential stratification between the priest and the parishioners, local people tell the story as though the priest were "one of their own", acting in their name, speaking their dialect, putting the empire in its place on their behalf.

Collisions in the 1990s are more complex in content, but they share the same essential quality of incommensurable forms of life running into each other in the same time/space. On Friday 15 March 1996, St Patrick's Bank Holliday weekend, at around 8.00 pm, Philip Sheedy, having had a few drinks in a pub in the Dublin suburb of Tallaght, got into his car (for which he had received the keys just the day before; he had little experience of driving) with a male friend. At around the same time, Anne (a stay-at-home mother) and John Ryan (a meat boner) from Tallaght, along with their two young children and a friend's child, were returning from a swimming trip. At 8.10 pm, Anne Ryan drove onto the Glenview roundabout in Tallaght; seconds later Sheedy's car "dropped out of the sky" onto her car. Sheedy had been driving at speed from another direction, lost control of his car, hit the centre of the roundabout, causing the car to "take off like a missile" flying 60 feet through the air, landing on the driver's side of the Ryan's car, killing Anne Ryan almost instantly. John Ryan suffered a fractured skull, a broken jaw, and a broken hand, while all three children escaped serious injury. Both Sheedy and his passenger were uninjured.[1]

This horrific collision has become a nexus around which the forces of collision culture have been played out. We are not saying here that Sheedy should not have been punished, but rather that the furore around this particular case illustrates the extent to which Sheedy became a target for collective anxieties about the socially destructive effects of the Celtic Tiger, portrayed as a prosperous young architect, drinking after work, colliding with and killing the mother of the working-class family bringing the kids home from the pool. In a sense, this event tapped into broader anxieties about aggressive individualism and its denial of constraints and responsibility which is a danger to us all. This sensibility is expressed in the current Irish idiomatic formulations that "things have gotten out of control", and that "we have lost the run of ourselves". Indeed, all of this is true, and tragically, horribly real, as this collision literalises. But the story is more complicated, and if we follow the thread of this story it can lead us into the heart of the labyrinth of contemporary Irish

---

[1] Compiled from newspaper reports and eyewitness accounts of the accident, from *The Irish Times, The Sunday Times, and The Sunday Business Post.* For comprehensive synopses and reviews of the Sheedy case and its aftermath, the O'Flaherty affair, see *Irish Independent,* Saturday, 17 April 1999; *Irish Examiner* 21 April 1999; *Irish Times,* 23 May 2000.

society, where we can confront the monster, and hopefully find our way safely back out again.

The Sheedy affair, as will become clear below, elaborates the theme of collision culture, as what it reveals is not simply the collision, but the pile-up: the cumulative effect of a variety of cultural collisions impacting upon one another. Furthermore, it illuminates the phenomenology of the collision: twisted wreckage and scattered debris litter the Irish cultural landscape. Social institutions and forms of life, like vehicles, are twisted and impacted into one another, such that amid the chaos it is difficult to discern to which social form — traditional/modern, local/global — the shattered glass and debris belongs. And there are many casualties and multiple injuries. Irish people, casualties of collision culture, are like accident victims: injured, maimed, in shock. Long after the debris has been cleared away from the scene, the collision still reverberates and survivors remain traumatised. This specific case is a particularly tragic example, and one cannot but sympathise with all of those involved. However, out analysis is intended to demonstrate that this tragic case is in a sense a lightning rod around which our collective emotions about change have distilled.

Philip Sheedy doesn't easily conform to his stereotype of upper-class privilege. His background is ordinary and familiar. His father worked as a supervisor with FÁS, a state agency established during the recessionary 1980s responsible for retraining workers made redundant and unemployed. Sheedy attended the Dublin Institute of Technology School of Architecture — not an ivy-league university, but an upwardly mobile technical college — and graduated in the early 1990s specialising in computer-aided design. After finishing his training he worked for an architect based in a midlands town, where he remained for two years. In 1996, he took up an appointment with the South Dublin County Architects' Department. Three months prior to the collision, he had taken up a new position within the Department as Assistant Architect, on a temporary contract, earning a relatively modest salary of £21,000 per annum. His job involved designing Local Authority (public) housing. At his trial, friends and character witnesses described him as "very diffident, very quiet, a serious and hardworking professional architect" and after the accident he was described as "extremely depressed, practically suicidal". During his trial, a community worker gave a character reference stating that Sheedy had done valuable voluntary work designing sheltered housing for a community project in the midlands.[2]

Though Sheedy had a licence and he was used to driving his parents' car, the car involved in the collision was the first car he owned. This is a telling detail. It shows that Sheedy's experience is that of delayed, and then accelerated, upward social mobility. He is in his late twenties, has been employed as an architect for several years already, but it is only now that he can afford his first car, a second-hand car; and an interesting car it is, a Ford Probe. A Ford Probe is an ambiguous vehicle, neither a thoroughbred sports car — a Porsche, for example — nor a family saloon, but something in between. Ford describes the Probe as having "Head-turning good looks, stirring 24-valve performance and breathtaking

---

2 From newspaper reports of the Sheedy trial, sources: ibid.

handling . . . a sports coupe as much fun to drive as it is beautiful to look at." "The moment you slide into Probe's sports contoured seats you feel in control. . . . The emphasis is clearly on performance driving. . . . Probe strikes an impressive balance between grip and ride comfort with a reassuring sense of road feel. The steering is precise, sharp and responsive, empowering you to put the car through its paces with confidence and inspiring predictability". Probe "is designed to help drivers avoid accidents in the first place and to help reduce the risk of serious injuries to occupants in the event of collision". The Probe's power is delivered in "a seamless, satisfying stream of acceleration . . . a rich, even powerband that is ideal for both overtaking and motorway cruising".[3]

Of course, the type of vehicle individuals choose to buy is often governed more by economy than by advertising rhetoric; however, our point is that cars are rapidly becoming symbols of power and mobility, in Irish society, but as this case so tragically indicates, without the attendant attention to responsibility. All cars appeal to such metaphors of power and control, however. The Ford Probe (the name "Probe" itself resonant of modernity's conquering relation to uncertainty and ambiguity) is the sublime object of ideology at the heart of the libidinal economy of accelerated modernisation, a commodity fetish that promises to transcend natural and social limitations, to reconcile contradictions. It is a desirable machine, perfectly designed for the desires of the young, newly but uncertainly affluent and insecurely individualised subject of contemporary Ireland. If socio-economic status is uncertain, the Probe has

---

[3] Ford Probe advertising brochure. Marketing Communications, Ford Motor Company Ltd., Brentwood, Essex, England, 1996.

luxury and class. If post-Catholic sexual and emotional inhibi-
tions and insecurities linger on, Probe's beautiful, distinct, purposive lines turns heads for us; it is an attractive, erotic, phallic
machine, with grip, feel, and ride comfort. If our being amongst
History's losers, if post-colonial historical impotence looms
large in our collective identity, Probe enables us to perform; it
has exhilarating power, to overtake, to cruise, to cut through
the air. If our new powers are doubtful and somewhat uncertain, Probe gives assurance, precise handling; it empowers, puts
you in control, in command. If we are inexperienced, if we experience accelerated modernisation as uneven, unsettling, and
perilous, Probe gives "experience beyond our expectations",
so that "acceleration is seamless, satisfying, and safe for the
occupants, even in the event of a collision".

The dark irony is breathtaking, and rather than being
merely coincidental, points to a deeper truth: that in Freud's
(1976) terms, the car is now the wish-fulfilling "dream machine" par excellence of the subject of collision culture. Philip
Sheedy is reviled not because of his excessive difference from
a traditional collective representation of ourselves as caring,
family-centred members of a responsible community, but
rather that the radically alien form of life that he seems to
represent is in fact not alien to us at all, but on the contrary
is completely familiar to us. The anger at Sheedy is individualised, but is also a symptom of Irish collective guilt for our
own excesses, and collective self-hatred and fear of what we
are becoming.

In the ten days before Sheedy was sentenced in October
1997, 28 people were killed in traffic accidents. The morning
he appeared in court, the newspaper headlines were of road

deaths. The judge said that the four-year sentence should reflect "the urgency of addressing the carnage on the roads".[4]

While Sheedy was imprisoned, sometime during October 1998 a friend of Sheedy's "bumped into" Hugh O'Flaherty, a Supreme Court judge, on the street near their respective homes on Morehampton Road, Donnybrook, a fashionable upmarket Dublin suburb.[5] As well as being a friend of Sheedy's friend's family, O'Flaherty is from the same home town as the then Minister for Justice, and has close associations with the governing Fianna Fáil party. As they chatted in the street, Sheedy's friend outlined the case to O'Flaherty, and the possibility of a temporary release for Christmas "came up". O'Flaherty "just nodded . . . he said he would get back to me". O'Flaherty responded to the commonness of the Sheedy story. His motives for becoming involved were "humanitarian", he says. Perhaps he recognised that Sheedy was not so much a monster as he was an ordinary young man caught up in the larger tragic drama of collision culture.

O'Flaherty contacted the Dublin County Registrar for the Circuit Court and "enquired about the conditions under which sentenced prisoners could have their sentence reviewed". He "mentioned" the Sheedy case and "suggested" that it may be possible to have the sentence reviewed. The Registrar said to O'Flaherty that indeed it would be possible. The Circuit Court Registrar then contacted Sheedy's solicitor, and asked when he was putting Sheedy's case up for review. The solicitor said he

---

[4] From newspaper reports of the Sheedy trial: *Irish Times, Sunday Times.*

[5] The O'Flaherty saga has been extensively covered by the Irish media. These details are taken from reports in *The Irish Times* and subsequent summary reviews, note 1 above.

knew nothing about a review, and would have to contact the Sheedy family and Sheedy's previous solicitor. He asked the Registrar what was going on. The Registrar replied, "You don't want to know." On 12 November 1998, Sheedy appeared before the Circuit Court where, after a brief hearing (neither the Gardaí not the Attorney General were represented, and the transcript is less than two pages), Justice Cyril Kelly suspended the remainder of his sentence. Twelve days later, Justice Kelly was promoted to the High Court.

Having been released, Sheedy returned to work in December 1998. Shortly afterwards, one of John Ryan's friends saw Sheedy going to work, and informed John Ryan. Ryan contacted another friend who was a Garda sergeant in Tallaght, who made inquiries and found that nobody knew how Sheedy had been released so early. The sergeant, acting as a member of the public, reported the matter to the Chief State Solicitor's office, while Ryan wrote to the Department of Justice enquiring as to how and why Sheedy was released. The Chief State Solicitor reported the matter to the Director of Public Prosecutions, who in turn informed the Attorney General. The Attorney General called to Chief Justice Hamilton at the Supreme Court, who summoned O'Flaherty. While the Chief Justice accepted that O'Flaherty became involved in the case in a spirit of humanitarian interest, his actions with regard to the case were "inappropriate and unwise" and compromised the administration of justice. Meanwhile, the story was reported in the media. In the ensuing controversy, O'Flaherty resigned from the Supreme Court.

There are a number of significant collisions here. First, various people bump and run into each other. Sheedy's friend bumps into the Supreme Court judge on the street; Ryan's friend runs into Sheedy on his way to work. Dublin is a modern metropolis, which is still like a small town. O'Flaherty, the Supreme Court judge, is a representative of the traditional political establishment in Ireland: a Fianna Fáil appointment — the party founded by de Valera — he is steeped in the tradition of clientelism and brokerage, where power brokers "pull strokes" (do favours) for constituents and friends in return for political support and legitimation.[6] This is so much the habitus of Irish political culture that very little actually needs to be said, verbalised, articulated, or explicated. Instead, things are "mentioned", or "come up in passing" in an otherwise casual conversation. In the reconstruction of the narrative in the national media, when a Supreme Court judge calls a Registrar of the Circuit Court, again, very little needs to be said. A case is mentioned, a general enquiry about review, and, if the media is to be believed, the Registrar fills in the blanks. This practice is familiar and well worn as a pattern of action, like a cow's path on the contour of the political landscape, a habit, a scheme, a way of doing things. The wheels are in motion, and the machine rolls on in the traditional pattern of action.

And then another collision: when the parish priest collided with the Royal Navy officer, the constitutive antagonism of the social was sutured by the hegemony of populist Catholic republicanism, but now the discursive field is opened up by competing discursive practices. The public sphere is more differentiated and cross-cut by antagonisms. The habitus and

---

6 See O'Carroll, J.P. (1987)

institutions of traditional Irish political culture collide with the emerging institutions of reflexive modernisation:[7] inquiries from members of the public to Government departments and the Attorney General's office, asking for explanations, seeking clarifications. This emerging form of late modern political culture collides with the traditional institutionalisation of legitimation based on favours performed by charismatic brokers. New rules and protocols infusing bureaucracy and officialdom, principles of accountability and transparency, collide with the institutional basis of clientelism, namely the opacity of institutions that renders clients dependent on brokers for access to power/knowledge. O'Flaherty was asked to account for his actions to the Government Committee for Justice, Equality and Women's Rights, a new body representing the increasing reflexive modernisation of Irish political institutions. A broader culture of mass media saturation, "the ecstasy of communication" (Baudrillard, 1987), collides with the institutionalised forms of privacy, secrecy, the understandings shared by members of organisations, professions, institutions that continue to function as though they were communities, on which a traditional political culture and habitus of action is based. However, as far as the media is concerned, one could go further and say that, in a situation where these institutions are operating in an uncertain climate, the media could be attempting to broker its own position of moral authority; the undermining of institutions is in the interests of the media.

---

[7] See Beck, U. "The re-invention of politics" in Beck, U., Giddens, A., and Lash, S. (1995). For a discussion related to Irish material see Keohane, K. (1999), "Reflexive modernisation and systematically distorted communications: an analysis of an Environmental Protection Agency hearing", *Irish Journal of Sociology*, Vol. 8, pp. 71–92.

O'Flaherty is the prototypical casualty of this pile-up, this multiplication of collisions between the institutions of traditional political culture and the emerging institutions of reflexive modernisation in Ireland. And tragically so. Unlike so many of the cases examined by the current Tribunals,[8] there is no question of bribery or personal gain in O'Flaherty's case. O'Flaherty is the traditional "man of honour" who exercises judgement and personally intervenes in the workings of the bureaucracy of the legal system, motivated, he claims, by humanitarian interests, not personal gain. Ironically, this charismatic broker is, as Weber (1978, vol. 2) emphasises, the only bulwark against the even grimmer prospect of domination by instrumental reason in the iron cage of rationalised acquisitiveness (1976).

Two years after O'Flaherty's resignation from the Supreme Court, the Minister for Finance of the Fianna Fáil government called personally to his home in County Kerry, to offer him an appointment as the Irish Vice-President of the European Investment Bank. After the collision and trauma comes the work of rehabilitation and the attempt to restore order. The traditional institutions of Irish political culture attempted to carry on business as usual. Despite public objection and a legal challenge to the appointment on the grounds of recent legislation on fairness and equity in appointments procedures, the Government was "determined to uphold the appointment". Eventually, in the midst of public controversy,

---

[8] Since the late 1990s there have been a number of tribunals investigating corruption in Irish public service. Those implicated have ranged from former Prime Ministers, Ministers, and senior Government figures, to minor officials in Local Government. The corruption revealed is of undisclosed payments to political parties and individual politicians, especially bribes from property developers for land zoning and planning decisions.

and as it became apparent that the directors of the European Investment Bank were unlikely to ratify the appointment,[9] O'Flaherty, still the man of honour, withdrew his own candidacy. In his place the Government nominated the Second Secretary of the Department of Finance, a career bureaucrat, a cog, as Weber laments, simply becoming a bigger cog in the inexorable process of mechanised petrification.[10]

As Zizek (1989) shows, in order to die, one has in fact to die twice: after the real death, there must be a symbolic death also. For example, in the case of the transformation of Eastern Europe, by the late 1980s communism was in reality already "dead", a spent force, an ideology and a form of life with no legitimacy, with no purchase on collective hearts and minds. But to become "really real", as it were, this death needed to be marked by a symbolic death: tearing down the Berlin wall, knocking over the great monuments of Marx, executing the tyrants and their former henchmen. Only by these second deaths could the old institutions come to realise for themselves that they were in fact dead, and could finally be laid to rest. Many of Ireland's traditional social forms have yet to experience this second death. "The old is dying and the new cannot be born. In this interregnum there are a great variety of morbid symptoms."[11]

---

[9] Amongst other things the EIB directors were concerned by the flood of e-mails from members of the Irish public to various EU offices objecting to O'Flaherty's appointment, underlining both the contexts of reflexivity and the ecstasy of communication impinging on the institutions and practices of contemporary governance.

[10] Weber, M. "Some consequences of bureaucratization", in L. Cozer and B. Rosenberg (eds) 1964 *Sociological Theory* New York: Macmillan

[11] Gramsci, cited by Offe (1984).

CHAPTER 3

Understanding Irish Suicides[1]

Suicide in Ireland has risen dramatically in the past decade. The increase is especially marked amongst men in their twenties. There is some evidence to suggest that the rise has been greater in rural areas.[2] The grim statistics are well known, and tragic stories of Irish suicides have become all too familiar. With the exception of Smyth, MacLachlan and Clare (2003), the public discourse on suicide in Ireland has been mostly informed by medical and psychological explanations, which analyse the epidemiology of suicide in terms of "risk factors", linking suicide with alcohol and substance abuse, for example, with mental illness such as depression, and with stress associated with transition to adulthood and role adaptation. Such an approach, while useful in understanding individual cases, has not contributed significantly to our understanding of why the overall pattern of death by suicide in Ireland

---

[1] Co-authored with Derek Chambers, National Suicide Research Foundation, Cork. Identifying details of the cases have been omitted and disguised to ensure anonymity.

[2] Kelleher, M.J., Chambers, D. and Corcoran, P. (1999), "Suicide and Religion in Ireland: An Investigation of Thomas Masaryk's Theory of Suicide", *Archives of Suicide Research* (5)173–180.

has changed over the past 20 years or so. Here we offer a sociological interpretation of Irish suicide, one that collects the bio-medical and psychological discourse in terms of a broader historical and cultural explanation. The interpretation is based on a number of case profiles compiled by Irish coroners, which we interpret within a sociological framework of transformation in Irish society. In these "sociological autopsies"[3] we show that the causes underpinning the increase in suicide in Irish society stem from the historical experience of cultural "collisions"; collisions between the vestiges of traditional community and accelerated modern society, between the rural and the urban, the local and the global; collisions that impact traumatically on the life histories of individuals. Suicides, we argue, are to be understood as the casualties of Ireland's "collision culture".

In a classic sociological study, Durkheim (1966) identifies four types of suicide: "altruistic" and "fatalistic" suicides, which he associates with pre-modern, traditional community, and "anomic" and "egoistic" suicides characteristic of modern society. Altruistic suicide is, for example, the obligatory suicide of widows in patriarchal Asia, the suicide of shamed warriors who dishonoured their people, the suicide of elderly tribespeople when they became a burden in times of scarcity. Altruistic suicide, suicide wherein people kill themselves for the group, is symptomatic of people's excessive immersion in collective life and their insufficient individuation. In contemporary contexts, exceptional instances such as mass suicide

---

[3] Chambers, D. (1999), *A Sociological Account of the Rise in Irish Suicide: Suicide as a Symptom of the Celtic Tiger*, unpublished MA dissertation, Dept. of Sociology, NUI Cork.

by cult members, kamikaze pilots, suicide bombers, and hunger strikers, patriots and martyrs who die for the Emperor, for their People, or for a Cause, are examples of altruistic suicide. "Fatalistic" suicide is, for example, the suicide of slaves, unwilling partners in loveless arranged marriages, people who are trapped and whose abilities to determine their own futures are cut off. Fatalistic suicide is indicative of the excessive moral regulation often found in pre-modern despotic cultures. The rare contemporary instances of fatalistic suicide would be concentration camp detainees, and perhaps heroin-addicted prisoners.

By contrast with altruistic and fatalistic suicides in pre-modern contexts, Durkheim identifies "egoistic" suicide as typical of modern society, for example the suicides of rock stars and celebrities. Egoistic suicide is symptomatic of the extent to which modern people are excessively individuated and insufficiently integrated with normal collective life. Mundane and sadly familiar examples of egoistic suicide may be suicides related to pressures and anxiety generated by expectations that we be "stars" ourselves, in examinations and career performances. Such suicides may increase during periods of disintegration of community when social supports are diminished. Although there has been a diminution of the strength of social ties and community in Irish society, egoistic suicide remains more characteristic of the larger, "anonymous" cities of continental Europe and North America.

The fourth type of suicide Durkheim identifies is "anomic" suicide, again associated with the conditions of modern society. Anomic suicide is suicide related to times of moral confusion due to rapid social change, when moral and regulatory frameworks and institutions are unstable. Anomic suicide is symptomatic of insufficient moral regulation, arising not only from the decline of a singular source of moral authority, but also from the proliferation of competing moralities, causing the normative confusion characteristic of modern life, and especially of periods of rapid transformation. In modern society suicides increase during periods of economic recession, as well as during economic booms, as these are both equally times of instability. In contemporary Ireland, anomic suicide is related not only to the boom, but also to the decline of Catholicism as a unifying moral framework, fundamental transformations of gender roles and family life, as well as the secular moralities of affluence — consumerism and materialism.

Durkheim's *Suicide* is part of a broader analysis of the social transformation of the nineteenth century, the emergence of a secular, urban, industrial society, and the tension between the new society and the vestiges of pre-modern, religious, rural and agrarian community. Durkheim (1984) draws up the characteristic and distinguishing features of pre-modern "traditional" community and modern society. In traditional community, there is an undifferentiated division of labour, whereas there is a high degree of occupational specialisation in modern society, with the corollary that one's resemblance to others is valued in the former, whereas one's specific and peculiar difference from others is valued in the latter. Traditional community is integrated by the principle of mechanical solidarity: the individual resembles the other members of the collective not only in terms of labour and occupation, but also shares the same body of beliefs, values and sentiments, which constitute a pervasive religious cosmology that is dense, clearly defined, and inflexible, a "*conscience collective*". By contrast, modern societies are integrated by organic solidarity: the person in modern society has an individual conscience that is differentiated and flexible, and they are individually morally responsible for their actions. When a member of a traditional community offends the collective they (and their kin, insofar as the individual is indistinguishable from the group) are repressively sanctioned, typically expunged from the collective body, whereas in modern society the deviant is required to make restitution; they are rehabilitated, reintegrated, and the smooth functioning of social life is restored.

Traditional community and modern society are fundamentally different forms of collective life and stand in contradistinction and opposition to one another. But the models of "traditional" and "modern" which Durkheim derives and elaborates are analytic abstractions, pure forms, or what Weber calls "ideal types", models which no particular society fully corresponds to, but which, rather, more or less correspond to and approximate instances and examples of collective life, enabling a sociologist to speak meaningfully about the substantive differences between the regulated patterns of action that constitute the characteristic features of particular societies. For example, Ireland, by comparison with other modern western societies, has been a relatively racially and culturally homogenous, strongly religious, rural community, but in a short period has been undergoing major social transformation. This process was accelerated in the 1990s due to the economic boom, but vestiges of traditional community co-exist uneasily and often collide with forms of life characteristic of modern society.

If one examines the rise in Irish suicides in terms of Durkheim's analysis and ideal-typologies, it can be argued that the
suicide rate in Ireland is closely correlated to broad structural
transformations of Irish society. Foremost of these is the economic boom, where relative material affluence is manifest psy-
chologically in a sense of boundlessness: the expansion of desires and the amplification of acquisitiveness to limitlessness
and insatiability. Insatiability, Durkheim (1974) says, is always a
sign of morbidity. Coinciding and closely intertwined with a
period of unparalleled economic expansion, is an unprecedented crisis in the Catholic Church in Ireland, which had
previously, for at least one hundred years, enjoyed a moral
monopoly (Inglis, 1998). The expansion of material horizons
and the decline of the moral authority of the Catholic Church
are the two primary sources of egoism and anomie in contemporary Ireland: banks offer extensive credit at low rates,
promoting loans with ads explicitly stating: "the sky's the
limit", buy "whatever your heart desires"; while the church,
eclipsed by materialism and commodity fetishism, and rocked
by scandal, has its moral role reduced to apologising for its
own excesses and abuses. Throughout the 1990s the Catholic
Church in Ireland has repeatedly been implicated in scandal,
ranging from prominent individual clergymen fathering children, to a large number of high-profile prosecutions of individual clergy and religious communities for child sexual abuse
and cruelty. Such phenomena have a long history in religious
institutions, and it is not merely coincidence that the Catholic
Church in Ireland is the subject of such exposure and prosecution at this particular historical conjuncture. Rather it reflects a new institutional configuration in which the sacred

authorities of community are eclipsed by the secular principles of society: central to this is a democratic and legal rational discourse of rights — rights of the individual in general, and the child in particular; a discourse of sexual equality, and associated measures to regulate the play of power, between men and women, between adults and children, especially in the realm of sexuality. These are influences linked to globalisation, from the political culture of North America and the legal institutions of the EU. These global discourses coincide with a local economic boom in Ireland that for the first time provides a large number of people with alternatives to the Catholic Church as a provider of material, cultural and spiritual needs.

Under these conditions of expansive individualism and the decline of a totalising and unifying religious worldview, we find ourselves, as Nietzsche (1967) says, "unable to find any limitation, any check, any considerateness within the morality at our disposal". There are other important transformations taking place also. Traditional gender roles and family forms collide with new alternatives (O'Connor, 1999). Young men, for instance, experience their traditional role privileges and securities as under threat or circumscribed by the influences of feminism and gender equality in employment. Young women experience the same changes, positively as an expansion of horizons (manifest in their lower suicide rates than men) but negatively as performance pressures, and an intensification of the stress to combine split roles: traditional homemaker, wife and mother; modern independent career woman.

While the accurate "mapping" of suicidal behaviour in any great detail has proved unreliable to date, anecdotal evidence would suggest that for our young people, the increase in the

rates of suicidal behaviour is most marked in country towns
— places that are neither villages where the fabric of community remains relatively intact, nor cities where conditions
of anomie have themselves become normalised. Contemporary Irish country towns are in-between places, neither rural
nor urban, hybrid, liminal places, characterised by uncertainty
and anomie.

The increase in the Irish suicide rate over recent years is a
textbook illustration of Durkheim's general thesis that the
social form within which modern suicide rates can be interpreted and understood is anomie — the loss of a central sta-
ble normative framework, the proliferation of competing, con-
fusing norms, an expansion of material and moral horizons,
and amplification of desires that in contexts of limitlessness
are insatiable; and egoism — the disintegration of traditional
social bonds of family, kinship, and community, the emergence
of the unbounded subject and the cult of the individual. But
we are concerned here with the particularity of suicide at this
current conjuncture of Irish society. While we may readily
perceive the general form by examining the suicide rate in
historical context, if we are to interpret and understand, as
Weber (1978) says, that which is "specific and peculiar" to the
phenomenon of suicide in contemporary Ireland — that is, if
we are to step into a person's shoes in order to understand
and interpret their actions, in this case the despairing, terrible
action of suicide — we need to get close, closer than may be
comfortable, to the phenomenon. To grasp and understand
what is specific with regards to the traumatic experience of
living in contemporary Ireland, we must focus more closely on
the idiomatic content of Irish suicides.

The first case we examine is that of a young man employed as a technician, found at his parents' house, having shot himself. His mother discovered her son's body after she had returned from a weekend away. She called her husband's office and then called a priest and Gardaí.

This young man, university educated and professionally employed, came from a wealthy urban family who had built a contemporary lifestyle based on country living in a rural retreat combined with frequent travel abroad. The incongruous element that reminds us that this is Ireland is that the young man is still living with his parents. Though employed and independent, he is not fully individuated and autonomous. In traditional Irish community it would have been quite common and normal for adult children — if they had not emigrated — to be still part of the nuclear household, but presently this domestic situation comes under pressure. Successful young men are expected to set up on their own, and to assume the burdens of home ownership and autonomy, even though, at the same time, adolescence extends into adulthood. There is also the added pressure of house prices, which are beyond the means of even moderately well-off young people. And there is a further incongruous and telling element: that for this apparently very modern Irish family it is the priest who is called upon immediately, not the gardaí or ambulance, the helpers for a modern emergency, but the bearer of the authority and succour of a traditional community.

Another case is that of a 35-year-old woman employed in a managerial position, living in a village in the greater Dublin area. She was married with children but had in the past lived with her lover — who was also her employer — for several months. When the affair had begun, her lover's wife began harassing her, and prior to death she had been taking medication for depression. On the night of her suicide, she left home saying she would visit her parents. Her husband phoned his father-in-law to say that she might call. She didn't call to her parents' house. Her husband reported her missing later that night. He also phoned her employer (her lover) who said that he would help in the search and also that he would ask another employee to help. Her husband found her body.

In this case the woman lives in a bewildering space between two opposed forms of life. She lives in what is no longer a village, but also not part of the city: a place Bonner (1997) calls a "rurban" area, typical of contemporary Ireland. On the one hand, she is a modern woman: employed outside the home, making her own choices about her love life, and kicking against the traces of conventional traditional morality of the social roles of wife and mother. On the other hand, she is still deeply immersed in traditional community. While she has a function in a modern economic division of labour, this does not give her autonomy, as she is also married with children. Further, her boss is also her lover, re-inscribing the intimate sphere within the market relation that freed her from the constraints of the family. She has no anonymity. Her husband knows of the affair, as does her lover's wife, from the beginning, as indeed do her own family and her in-laws, and all are in communication with one another. On the night of her death her husband calls her parents, and her lover, to report her missing. Her lover/boss in turn calls another employee, also familiar with the situation, to help. There is a dense network of social relations, a community to call upon for assistance.

The woman is sufficiently individuated to experience and acknowledge her own desires, and to act on them, and yet she is insufficiently free to act on them with autonomy, privacy, and impunity. She lacks not only the anonymity of city life, but also its plurality: in a village in the greater Dublin area, even in twenty-first-century Ireland, there are few women with whom she might share a common experience. Divorce, and life after divorce for women in their thirties with children, is not institutionalised as "normal", as it might be in a North American or European city. It is likely that she has no peer group, no support, no models to follow. She is on her own. Torn between desires and constraints belonging to two separate forms of life, her desire to be free and her obligation to herself to be autonomous, and equally, her desire to "do the right thing", to fulfil her obligations as a good wife, mother, and daughter, to simultaneously perform two sets of roles belonging to the divergent moral orders of traditional community and modern society that exist simultaneously in contemporary Ireland. The tragic depths revealed in this story comes through in the way in which the people involved are quite obviously trying to do their best to cope with the difficult situation. Her husband, her parents, and her lover are in communication. They are motivated by their mutual care for her, but it is perhaps this very mutuality, a mutuality no doubt charged with a potent mixture of love and anger, envy and desire, that formed the small terrible world that became unbearable for her.

In each of the cases examined here, we are trying to gain "an understanding of the larger historical scene in terms of its meaning for the inner life and the external career of a variety of individuals". As C. Wright Mills (1959) says, "neither the life [or the death] of an individual nor the history of a society can be understood without understanding both". Behind every suicide there is a realm of private trouble, an individual tragedy; a husband, wife, mother, father, son or daughter, a friend or neighbour; a life lost, others' lives shattered. Behind a note left by the next suicide case is a painful and traumatic individual story of conjugal anomie, unhappiness, recrimination, paranoia, fear, hatred, revenge and pain. But a sociological imagination may help us to see and understand the ways in which biography and history are intertwined, so that private troubles are in fact symptoms of public issues. The tragic drama played out in the life-worlds of individuals constitutes a microcosm of the larger tragic drama of collision culture in contemporary Ireland.

In this case, we have a suicide note in which a husband rages at his wife's alleged infidelity, and the shame and hurt that he says she has caused. He feels this acutely, intolerably. But to feel this shame implies that he feels himself to be a part of a community that shares a morality, a normative framework, a "*conscience collective*"; a community that "knows what you have done", a community that watches and sees what its members are doing, that discusses these actions, that judges these actions against normative standards and values that it holds dear, and that imposes repressive sanctions, of ostracism, of humiliation, of shame, on those who transgress these cherished values. This man feels himself to be a part of such a social order. He cannot go into the local pub, for fear that "people are talking about me, laughing at me behind my back". He is furious at his wife, for "messing around", messing up the ideal of the traditional family that he feels subject to, that he used to feel they were both once beholden to, that she has violated. His rage is directed against her for violating a collective agreement, shared by them both and by a wider community. He is vengeful, and he tries to punish her through his own death, as he hopes that by such a desperate shameful act (shameful within the traditional normative framework in which he lives, and in which in his despair he thinks his wife also still lives) his wife will be shamed; she will be seen, and see herself as having "done it"; that she will be held responsible, and hold herself responsible to the community for his death. He invokes the collective moral authority of the traditional community to be a power that might torment and crush his estranged wife. But the horrible irony, that may yet make his terrible act of vengeance impotent and absurd, he himself seems to sense. That she is estranged; that she is no longer a member of the traditional community that he feels himself so painfully to be a part of. He suspects a dreadful truth: that she can ignore them, and him; that she will "put [her] head in the sand and hide from the shame and hurt". He suspects that, unlike himself, she enjoys much greater moral autonomy, and is not subject to the traditional repressive sanction of shame. It is this half-realised knowledge that his wife and himself live in different worlds, governed by different normative frameworks, that underpins the extremes of desperation and cruelty in the timing of the act, at Christmas. Even if, as he suspects, she may not be subject any longer to the moral authority of the traditional community, she still belongs to a wider symbolic order in which Christmas will continue to be an important event, so he inserts the horror of his act at this point, deliberately intending to corrupt Christmas and irreparably damage the symbolic order for his wife and her family for ever.

Another suicide note, left by a young man in a midlands town,, again is a symptom of ambiguity and ambivalence characteristic of the collisions between vestigial tradition and accelerated modernisation in contemporary Ireland. The note contains a clear articulation of the idea of the good life that this young man claims he desired — "an ordinary life" — understood in terms of the values of a traditional community: the nuclear family, that he be breadwinner and provider for a wife and children. This is not an extravagant desire, but is nonetheless a dream belonging to a worldview that is being eclipsed even as he rearticulates it; a worldview that now competes with other, often opposed, imperatives: to be independent and unencumbered, to have a successful career, to not be tied down to boring conventions. This young man is halfway to having what he thought he desired, it seems — a loving relationship that "gave him the best few years of his life" — and yet even as he has what he thinks he desires, it seems to slip away from him, or, rather, he feels that unwillingly, he pushes and drives it away by his "selfishness".

On the one hand, he understands his suicide as somehow altruistic; he feels obliged to kill himself for the good of his community, and he feels answerable to that community even in death. He doesn't want "to ruin things for others" he says; people don't deserve the trouble he gives them, he wants people to be happy. He is sorry for trouble he feels he has caused, and for the pain he feels his death will cause. On the other hand, the note is symptomatic of the excessive egoism of modern culture. He feels himself to be responsible — all

too responsible — for the problems of his community: "I ruined . . . I've hurt people . . ., I'm sorry, . . . I wish I could
show you . . . I don't want to ruin everything . . . I've made
my decision . . . I must walk my path." The centrality of the
ego and the sense of individual conscience are striking here,
and coexist incongruously with his otherwise strong indica-
tions of social integration. In the collision culture of contemporary Ireland, the person exists in an anomic and egoistic
world where vestiges of the ideal forms of traditional community still haunt and hold sway over people, even as new
forms, new ideas, new collective representations, not yet
clearly formed, swirl into view; and a world which demands
action and choices be made, and responsibilities assumed by
an individual ego, even as that ego is still integrated by the
altruistic bonds of the community's *conscience collective*.

This strange and dreadful, paradoxical and profoundly
ambivalent situation of the person subject to the collision
culture of contemporary Ireland emerges in the two typical
cases we will now examine. The first is exemplified in a very
brief note left by a young man for his parents. It says, simply,
that he is sorry for the hurt his death will cause, but that he
hopes his insurance money will pay back some of what he
owes them, and will pay for a nice holiday for them both.

The second is the type of suicide, a small but significant
category, in which a vehicle accident is used to disguise suicide. This is obviously a very difficult case to prove in any particular instance, and of course that this means of suicide be so
difficult to establish with certainty is an intrinsic aspect of the
phenomenon — it is intended to disguise the deliberate action as accidental. One of Ireland's leading suicidologists

notes the incidence, suggesting that five per cent of single-vehicle road deaths are suicides,[4] and this is supported by anecdotal evidence from Gardaí and other researchers. The case illustrated and typified by the brief note left by the young man above differs from the car crash suicide in the obvious way that the first is not disguised. There is no explanation — nothing to be said, or too much to say — and yet the note is eloquent of a certain troubled reality — the ambivalent influences of egoism and altruism. Although the young man does not feel obliged to account for his action, to explain himself, indicating his sense of individuation and moral autonomy, at the same time he feels himself to be part of a network of economic and financial relations that he is obliged to reciprocate. He has to "pay back", and this is most conveniently done through the universal medium of modern social relations, money, made all the more impersonal as it is the insurance premium. And yet, this is by no means a simple cash settlement for debts incurred in the material economy of the household budget; for it is also clearly a gift, from a loving son to his parents. Gift exchange is the fundamental social relation (Mauss, 2002) and here the gift, a token of reciprocal affection in a wider libidinal economy of the unfathomable primordial web of mutual obligations that constitute family life, demonstrates with excruciating poignancy how this man is enmeshed in that web, even as he falls or breaks through it.

The suicide disguised as a car accident is symptomatic of the same profound ambivalence underpinning the experience

---

[4] Dr John Connolly, Mayo County Chief Psychiatrist, Secretary of the Irish Association of Suicidology, 1999. Connolly, J.F., Cullen, A. and McTigue, O. (1995), "Single Road Traffic Deaths — Accident or Suicide?" *Crisis*, (16)2.

of living in Ireland today. The car is quintessentially the *sine qua non* of a young man's independence in the symbolic order and imaginative structure of modern society. Yet it is frequently the parents' car that is the vehicle in question. Road traffic accidents disguise suicides and thus avoid the stigma of suicide for family and community. The suicide is individuated sufficiently (excessively) to make the act possible, and yet is simultaneously still sufficiently (excessively) integrated in communal life to feel obliged to save the family from shame and stigma. Not alone that, but as in the case above, there is an economic consideration of the insurance payoff, which again is both intended as a cash settlement, and as a "parting gift" in a fundamental traditional communitarian form in which gift-exchange is still formative, constitutive, reciprocal and obligatory.

Finally, the risk of suicide amongst young Irish farmers can also be interpreted in terms of the anomic and egoistic conditions under which modern farming is performed. In traditional Irish rural community, saving the hay, and indeed many routine harvesting practices, were communal, threshing perhaps most famously. This involved neighbouring farmers pitching in with one another's work, on the system of assured reciprocation, involving shared use of man, woman, and child power, tools, and indeed resources of association and sociability, food, refreshments, music, song, drink and dances on completion of work. Such events were in addition to the "*scoraíochting*", visiting one another's houses, doing the rounds of the parish, which went on during the year. Modern agricultural technologies and commercial practices do away with all of this. Silage, for example, means that farmers no longer have to come together to avail of a narrow window of opportunity to "make hay while the sun shines", and collective use of machinery and manpower is eliminated by the silage contractor. The most basic sociability is removed from this scenario. The contractor is frequently a "stranger", which in itself may bring sociable advantages,[5] but that possibility of enjoying the gift of difference which the stranger may bring is eliminated; the silage contractors usually work 24-hour shifts, with machinery drivers working alone and monotonously in air-conditioned sound-proofed cabs with hi-fi systems, scarcely coming into contact with one another, never mind with the modern farmer or his family, as they move swiftly from farm to farm minimising down-time to maximise profitability. All of the rural, traditional forms of sociation are swept away, leaving a social void so that the modern young Irish farmer who, though he is born into and tied to the land after the traditional pattern, experiences farming practice decreasingly as a meaningful totality, a way of life, and increasingly as merely an occupation, a job, as atomised and alienating as any other; and moreover, as a job in which there is "no future". The hyper-rationalisation of contemporary agribusiness has meant that small and medium-sized farms, which comprise some 70 per cent of Irish farms, are no longer economically viable. Irish family farms become hollow worlds where there is neither a past nor a future, and young farmers, like prisoners and drug addicts, experience themselves as being trapped in an unchanging present and become prone to a contemporary form of fatalistic suicide.

---

[5] "The Stranger" in Simmel (1971c).

Conclusion

Every individual case history of suicide has a personal story behind it, a story of depression, of pressure and performance anxiety related to exams or career, a story of marital disharmony, of alcohol or drug abuse, and so on. Medical and psychological discourses can identify the contributory factors that commonly recur, mapping an epidemiological pattern of typical cases. Such explanations of immanent factors in Irish suicide can be complemented by and enhanced with an explanation of transcendent causal factors. A fuller explanation of the increase in the Irish suicide rate is possible if we situate suicides in a broader sociological framework that transcends the life-world of the individual. A sociological perspective enables us to see that private troubles of milieu are related to public issues; that the case history of a suicide victim is part of a broader historical social pathology. Sociology identifies the characteristic general pathologies of modern society that lead to suicide as egoism and anomie. These problems are exacerbated in Ireland in particular as they coincide and collide with vestigial traditional social forms. Suicides are particularly florid symptoms of the prevalence of this social pathology, as it manifests itself at the level of the individual's life in contemporary Irish society.

CHAPTER 4

Case Studies in the Localisation of the Global: Celebrity in Contemporary Irish Culture

ON A VISIT TO GALWAY, OUR DAUGHTER wanted to go to McDonalds, which in fact was Supermacs, an import-substitute "Irish-owned family restaurant", indistinguishable from McDonald's in every substantial respect. The confusion of McDonald's and Supermac's, even to the keen eyes of a child, epitomises a broad historical process of homogenisation of Irish culture and identity wherein the local is transformed so that it resembles the global: the localisation of the global. Later the same day, she recognised a Claddagh ring as "the ring Angel gave to Buffy" (the Vampire Slayer). The Claddagh ring, an artefact with a genealogy particular to Galway, has become a floating signifier of traditional local culture, appropriated by the global culture industry to give connotations of anchorage in community and a sense of historical continuity to brooding, transcendentally homeless Los Angeleans (LA is the setting of the *Buffy* spin-off *Angel*) and is thus an attempt to embrace a particular, localised identity, perhaps as a buffer against global contexts devoid of particularity.

To repeat the argument which is at the core of this book, Irish social structures and institutions, culture and identity, are being transformed by processes of globalisation: technologies and markets of production, distribution and consumption generated by transnational corporations; administrative systems, governmental strategies and legal-rational principles developed by post-national and transnational institutions. At the same time, our social structures and institutions are shaped by the re-localisation of the global: local institutions, communitarian norms and principles of action translate and rework exogenous processes of globalisation, attuning them and making them consonant with local institutions. Irish culture and identity is characterised by the ambiguous and paradoxical ways in which the globalisation of the local and the re-localisation of the global are played out, sometimes in concert, sometimes colliding, in a social field crosscut with antagonism.

The local and the global, community and society, tradition and modernity, are not forms of life that supersede one another in linear historical progress, but that exist contemporaneously and interpenetrate with one another, collide and collude with one another, in the time/space of contemporary Ireland. Borders and boundaries between local and global, community and society, tradition and modernity are permeable. We have a foot in both — in many! — camps, and the experience of living in contemporary Ireland is that of living in an in-between world, in-between cultures and identities, an experience of liminality. The experience of modernisation and modernity in Ireland is ongoing, uneven, and fed by many sources; a multifarious and variegated experience, and hence perhaps best understood in terms of Bauman's (2000) notion of "liquid modernity". Liquescence expresses the idea that there is no such thing as modernity, the modern world, or a singular linear process of modernisation, which brought it into being; instead there are modernities, multiple modernities. There are also multiple traditions, for "traditional" and "tradition" are modern ideas, the world as defined retrospectively by modernity as the pre-modern, a "constitutive outside" with which modernity gains a positive ontology and definition of form. Thus, a mélange of modernities and traditions co-exist, interpenetrate and collide with one another in contemporary Ireland.

In this chapter we will examine celebrity in Irish popular culture, and specifically the representation of celebrity in the *RTÉ Guide* as an example of collision culture. The collision is the central unifying metaphor which expresses changes in Irish society today: "collisions" between the traditional and the modern, between the local and the global, between community and society, and between the values of collectivist and individualist worldviews. What we hope to show is that the traditional communalism and more modern forms of individualism each have positive and negative dimensions, and are impacting upon one another in interesting and diverse ways in Irish culture today as a result of the forces of globalisation.

The Celebrity as an Expression of the "Cult of the Individual"

One of the most marked effects of globalisation has been to promote the values of individualism against those of community. According to Durkheim (1984) the division of labour — occupational specialisation — means that people become valued not for their resemblance to the group (their belonging to family and kin, parishes, villages, their sharing the same beliefs and values as others) but for directly opposite reasons. Increasingly individuals are valued as individuals, for their uniqueness and peculiarity, for their specialness and irreplaceability. The primary arena in which this can be seen is in the labour market, where one's value, in both quantitative and qualitative terms, that is, in terms of salary and status, is determined by the unique skills and abilities that one brings to the marketplace. Traditional bases of occupational stratification and life chances — to whom one is related ("pull" in our Irish idiom), one's gender — matter increasingly less. In the contemporary Irish labour market, the essential criteria of entry and advancement are technical and professional qualification and expertise. This systematic erasure of the vestiges of traditionalism, the prejudices of nepotism and patriarchy, what Durkheim calls forms of forced division of labour, is one of the primary tendencies pushing towards the equalisation of social relations in Ireland today.

However, this individuation of Irish society has had both positive and negative effects. Along with this formal equalisation through educational qualification and similar progressive developments, Durkheim (1984, 1974) sees some ominous tendencies, most notably for our interests here, the "cult of the individual". As one's unique and individual qualities become the source of value in the occupational arena, individuality in all aspects of life become valued and celebrated. This has ambiguous and paradoxical consequences. On the one hand, it is the basis of the new-found freedoms of contemporary Ireland: freedom of thought and expression; freedom of consciousness. But it is simultaneously the source of egoism and anomie, the characteristic pathological tendencies of modern society, discussed elsewhere in this volume in terms of suicide in Ireland. The cult of the individual is expressed throughout contemporary Irish culture and identity. For example, the eclipse of the idea of "the hero" by "the celebrity". But as with all of the phenomena of Ireland's collision culture, the new forms are not clearcut breaks with the past, but hybrid fusions in which vestiges of earlier social forms live on and are reproduced in what at first appear to be new institutions of Irish culture and identity.

Each and every society constructs an ideal type member who embodies and represents the values and virtues of their society, Durkheim (1974) says. The ideal type member is the model that others aspire to emulate and is the cornerstone of the entire social order. In traditional society, the hero is worshipped because he fights on our behalf. Irish culture, up until quite recently, has been brimming with heroes — usually martyred heroes — who fought for Ireland. The celebrity is worshipped because they "fight" for themselves, and in modern society the cult of the individual is manifest in the social form of the celebrity as ego ideal wherein we vicariously satiate our own desire for individual success. But consider the contrast, and the continuity, between Irish traditional heroes and heroines, our champions who fought on our behalf, who span the spectrum from Cuchulainn and Fionn MacCumhail to Daniel O'Connell and Michael Collins, from Countess Markiewicz to Mary Robinson, and contemporary celebrities who span the spectrum from Tony O'Reilly to Ronan Keating. In the case of the latter two "celebrities", whose pursuit is strictly egotistical calculation for private gain, we continue to lionise them as though they were heroes whose exploits somehow elevate us all. Similarly, there is continuity between "the Boys", the collective, generic name for heroic Irish insurrectionaries (who remain nameless, non-individualised — "the boys of Wexford", "the boys of Kilmichael"), and Boyzone and the celebrity status of members of "boy bands". Celebrity boys' faces and names are prominent, and their "personalities" are extravagantly exteriorised in biographies, "frank" interviews, and "intimate" photo-sessions, but as undifferentiated collectives, and even families — Boyzone, Westlife, the Corrs — who are not merely celebrities, but *Irish* celebrities, heroic for their victories on the global battlefields of the UK Charts and the MTV awards. Even Bono (whose heroic status is somewhat ambiguous because of his contrived stage persona, and whose self-presentation is consistent with that of the individualised, global celebrity elite) can be considered a hero because of his campaigns for justice in Africa and elsewhere.

The popularity of Irish talk radio is in part due to its dual function of celebrating modern individualism and simultaneously reconstituting traditional community, in articulating a unified sense of the "common good" despite the fragmenting, individualising effects of modernity and the plurality of worldviews recent social transformations have engendered. The celebrity "personality", typically the media personality — Gay Byrne, Marian Finucane, Pat Kenny — embodies the ideal of fully actualised individualism in modern society, but in Ireland these people are simultaneously "household names", embodiments of the idea of community.

Gay Byrne's *Late Late Show*, frequently celebrated as the herald of secular liberal cosmopolitan Irish society, equally interpellated traditional community. A characteristic feature of the show was the quintessential primordial form of community binding, namely gift exchange. In every show in exchange for "your being so good to come all the way to Dublin [from some little village in Mayo]" (the audience's gift is their presence, attention, and applause) Byrne always had a gift, "something for everyone in the audience".

As well, Irish talk radio individuates, elicits and celebrates individual listeners' diverse views, related to Gerry or Marian — always on an intimate, personal, first-name basis; as Andy Warhol predicted, in modern Ireland as in New York city, everyone gets 15 minutes of fame. But simultaneously the heroic work of the Irish talk show host as a "good listener" is to re-collect the audience as a community; individual people, who despite their often diverse views, share common values: "we" the modern Irish public, are all, still, basically, neighbours and friends "concerned" with this issue/problem that "affects us all". Thus Irish talk radio is a strong representation of the localisation of the global: it is a forum which both articulates and reflects on the recent changes in Irish society, and which reinscribes a notion of the collective onto the increasingly differentiated and globalised "voice(s) of the people".

Ambivalence towards Celebrity in the RTÉ Guide

Despite the fact that it is a manifestation of the "cult of the individual", however, the celebrity as an object of our collective gaze enables us to articulate a unified sense of the "common good" in the context of the fragmenting, individualising effects of modernity. Celebrities sometimes function as "lightning rods" whose stardom is perceived to have amplified or made visible particular negative aspects of their societies. As the examples below show, it is often their early deaths which "seal in" this mythological aspect of their celebrity, both in its "good" and "bad" manifestations. For instance, Marilyn Monroe and Elvis Presley are still objects of public fascination by a nostalgic global public: small town innocents who succumbed to overdoses of drugs, food or alcohol in the context of the loneliness and anomie of stardom, they function in the collective imaginary as symbols of the decline of American society, as some of the archetypical sacrificial victims of its hyper-individuation, egoism, mass consumption and excess. The intense outpouring of grief at the death of Princess Diana can also be seen as a public identification with her as the victim of an archaic and rigid royal family, and thus as a symptom (which is manifesting itself at many levels of the social hierarchy) of the decline of British civilisation. However, locating these celebrities within particular national social and cultural context is not to say that either these celebrities' fans, or the particular nature of their traumas, are limited to their countries or cultures of origin. Diana is also perceived as a victim of a globalisation insofar as she was hounded by the celebrity-seeking media, and was quite literally the victim of a collision of worlds where royalty meets celebrity in a high-speed car chase through Paris in order to evade the "paparazzi". In this sense, celebrity itself is paradoxical: the celebrity is conceived and shaped by both local and global desires, audiences, traumas and representations.

As the inquiries in the wake of Diana's death have illustrated, the media approach to celebrities is often invasive, voyeuristic and cruel. The stock-in-trade of mass magazines such as *Hello*, *OK*, *Now*, and numerous others is the elevation and denigration of celebrities, as is particularly evident in the recent treatment of the Beckhams. Movie "stars", media "personalities", public "figures" and the vestiges of "Royalty" are simultaneously lionised and "brought down to earth", alternately by the representation of the ideal of blissful perfection of the "royal wedding" and the "candid snapshot" of celebrities in unflattering poses (e.g. Princess Diana on an exercise machine and Jerry Hall revealing her cellulite in a bikini) when caught unawares. The underbelly of this culture — as exemplified in the tabloids — is the obsessive quest to catch these celebrities out. Mass audiences of popular culture are familiar with this ambivalent representation of celebrity, as "news" and as entertaining spectacle, and we orient to celebrities and their representations ironically. We may know very well that they are fabulous constructions of dream machines and spin doctors, but still we need the ideals that they represent, as they are central to modern living: ideals of perpetual youth and beauty, individuality, fame, success, wealth, power and influence. And yet as these ideals are more often than not far beyond the reach of ordinary people's everyday lives, just as we need the celebrity to represent them for us, we need to deflate the ideal, cut it down to size, so that we are not in thrall to it. The short-cut to profaning the secular equivalent of the sacred realm — the realm of the "stars" — is to knock the celebrities off their pedestals. Thus, the relation to celebrity in modern society is ambivalent, and the representation of celebrity in popular culture is that the celebrity is simultaneously elevated and debased.

In contrast to the dominance of American and British celebrity coverage in international magazines such as *Hello, OK* and *Now*, and perhaps to the invasive approach of some members of the international "paparazzi", Irish magazines have tried to maximise coverage of Irish celebrities and thus to corner the Irish market through a variety of different formulas. For instance, *VIP* has retained the *Hello* formula of depicting celebrities on their estates, in glamorous clothes, and at elite events (and thus has replicated its association of celebrity with wealth and beauty, if not youth) but with the entertainment and entrepreneurial elite of Ireland rather than Hollywood stars and European royalty. In contrast, the *RTÉ Guide*, Ireland's biggest-selling magazine, has adopted a more original formula of depicting Irish celebrities in terms of their commitment to family, work and community rather than on the basis of more superficial qualities of youth and beauty, which is perhaps a factor maintaining its readership in the face of stiff external competition with regards to celebrity coverage. In the *RTÉ Guide*, what is celebrated is Irish celebrities' heroic ability to maintain qualities of unpretentiousness and ordinariness in spite of their fame and the forces of the global culture industry.

The *RTÉ Guide* is Ireland's biggest-selling magazine because of its highly successful development of a niche market wherein the globalisation of the local and the re-localisation of the global are articulated and the ambivalence between modern individualism and traditional community are reconciled in the hybrid form of the "Irish celebrity" who is represented simultaneously as a unique individual and at the same time "one of our own". Irish stars are invariably represented by the *Guide* as principled, hard-working, modest, tenacious, and in control of their media image. Marian Finucane is applauded for being "exactly the same on air as in real life". The closing summary of an article on the band Westlife claims "It is obviously gonna take more than a couple of tornadoes to blow this group away" (17 June 2000, p. 4). As well, several cover stories feature an Irish "star" — Gaybo, Pat Kenny, or someone in one of the home-grown soaps, some "hot" new addition to the cast of *Fair City* — who, in the course of an interview framed as an intimate chat amongst friends, assures us that the cast of the show, or RTÉ as a whole, is a nice happy family, a microcosm of the community of Irish life, with values and vices that we all share and love. And another obligatory feature: the profile of the Irish Hollywood star, Pierce Brosnan, or "your man" from *Michael Collins*, who reassure us that although they live amongst the stars (and so vicariously we all share their elevation) their hearts belong to Ireland. The profile reveals them to be "grand ordinary lads", "down to earth", and "one of our own". This is especially so if they have become famous for playing the Other better than the other: Brosnan is a favourite because he is a better James Bond than the Englishman Roger Moore was.

More explicitly, this celebration of the local is usually achieved through a devaluation of the global, or life outside Ireland. In an interview with RTÉ Foreign Affairs correspon-dent Mark Little, the barrenness of his successful life as a Washington correspondent is clearly juxtaposed to the fulfil-ment of life in Ireland. His life in America is rhetorically ren-dered equivalent to one particular anecdote where he felt lonely and disconnected while stuck in an airport hotel lounge in contrast to his new, "more normal life in Dublin". Similarly, his critique of the "venom" of public debate in Ireland is not attributed to Ireland, but rather displaced outside, for "US-type apathy is creeping in here" (13–20 January 2001, p. 5).

In a similar vein, many articles eschew individual achievement in favour of everyday values of community and family: Sonia O'Sullivan's hard work and success is equated with the traditional role of an Irish woman: "Her mothering skills are obviously as effortless and as natural as her running ability" (26 August – 3 September 1999, p. 4). The paradox of Irish celebrity is that the notion of the "star", and the cult of individualism on which it is based, are fundamentally antithetical to some of the principles underpinning Radio Telefis Éireann, radio and television for the Irish community, that is public service TV committed to endorsing the values and the ethos of Ireland. RTÉ is torn between the objectives of reinscribing the symbolic boundaries of Irish community, and doing this through a medium that prioritises the individual over the collective, the transnational over the national. Paradoxically, Irish stars themselves are used to reinscribe the symbolic boundaries of the Irish community. Celebrity is acknowledged as the dominant social form, and is ritualistically paid homage to, but at times with criticism, and even as it is torn down there is an attempt to usurp and appropriate the form, to incorporate it into the collective body.

This ambivalence is expressed in a content analysis of the *RTÉ Guide* from the years 1999–2000, which reveals that the *Guide* simultaneously tries to reassert the priority of the collective over the individual while at the same time championing Irish celebrities at the expense of non-Irish celebrities, who are frequently depicted as morally or intellectually vacuous. The celebration of Irish celebrities in the *Guide* represents an important process of self-affirmation, which aids in recognising the achievements of Irish actors, musicians and radio personalities in the context of the cultural emergence of Ireland on the global stage. However, as we illustrate below, the *Guide* at times devalues non-Irish celebrities on fairly spurious grounds, and frequently for "excessive individuation" or tries to "domesticate" the non-Irish celebrity by casting them as individuals who, though rich and famous, truly desire what we Irish see ourselves as having: a form of life morally anchored by values of family and community.

Whereas non-Irish magazines such as *Hello*, *OK* and *Now* uniformly and voyeuristically seek to reveal flaws (such as marital squabbles or physical imperfections) of all stars regardless of nationality, the *Guide* is often very critical of non-Irish or particularly American stars, and specifically for expressing sexuality or individuality. An examination of the *RTÉ Guide* in the years 1999–2001 reveals the following standard features: an RTÉ reporter flies out to an interview in a hotel or studio in Los Angeles, New York, or London, to conduct reviews or interviews with Hollywood stars, in which the star is shown by the RTÉ reporter to be deficient in some way. For instance, Catherine Zeta-Jones Douglas's hope that her new family can live with some privacy prompted the response "She's just going to have to stop trading in that star status then, isn't she?" (*RTÉ Guide*, November 2001). Gossipy snippets concerning affairs, and/or drug/alcohol problems are the fare here; for example, innuendoes that Matthew Perry has fallen off the prescription drugs wagon. There is also an implicit censorship of celebrities in terms of a traditionalist discourse of sexuality, and for women, a sexual double standard. For example, an article on David Bowie, an icon of both individualism and subversive sexuality, and his Somali model wife, ends with "Goodness me, if that's what they are like, then a small stack of disposable nappies in the hot press and the 3.00 am feed will do them the world of good" (*RTÉ Guide*, 4–10 March, 2000, p. 69). Bowie and Iman's transgression in the preceding interview was to claim that they still have sexual passion for each other. In one column of "Who's On", it is implied that Sharon Stone's on-screen sexuality, and specifically her below-the-waist nudity in *Basic Instinct*, means it is impossible that she be, as is claimed, a Mensa member with a high IQ (20–26 January, 2001). Stars perceived as "down-to earth", who avoid the limelight, such as George Clooney and John Cusack are treated more kindly. This raises the question as to whether or not women are treated more harshly than men because their celebrity status challenges assumptions about women's traditional role in the home.

What is unique, peculiar, and idiosyncratic in the Irish representation of non-Irish stars in the *RTÉ Guide* is that it is not conducted in terms of the collective representation (the idea) of the star in terms of perpetual youth and beauty, but in terms of normative standards of Irish society. Thus, while *OK* might focus on a star's appearance or weight gain, the *RTÉ Guide* focuses instead on her unfulfilled dreams of mother-hood, or her loneliness and lack of friends, as motherhood and community are more familiar ideals to an Irish readership than perpetual youth. If non-Irish stars are depicted in a neu-tral or even positive light, it is because they share perceived Irish values of family and community, or because they are lack-ing what we perceive we have. Jennifer Anniston may be rich and famous, but the article focuses entirely on her recent rift with her mother: "So, as Jennifer relaxes in her mansion in the

Hollywood hills, the rest of us can muse that no matter how many satellite links, e-mails, faxes, pagers, voice-mails and answering services we acquire, communication between human beings can stand a lot of improvement" (*RTÉ Guide*, 11–17 March 2000, p. 6). Jennifer Lopez may be gorgeous, and may have her posterior insured for a reputed $300 million (and her body for one billion), but what she really wants is a baby. Michelle Pfeiffer may have starred in many blockbusters, but the headline for her interview reads, "Being a Mom is my toughest role" (8–14 April 2000).

This is not to say that there is a one-to-one correspondence between the content of the *Guide* or a "dominant cultural attitude" of its readership, for individuals who read the *Guide* (i.e. Irish people) are a demographically and attitudinally diverse group, many of whom undoubtedly read ironically, critically, playfully and instrumentally (some may only read it to get TV listings!). Nor is it to contest the extent to which such representational affirmative action is an implicit critique of the ideology of meritocracy in America, and specifically of the way in which "successful" entertainers in America are clearly accorded a disproportionate degree of monetary reward, power and privilege, a symptom more generally of the polarisation between rich and poor, and of the prioritisation of entertainment over social improvement. Rather, our analysis is intended to bring to light some questions about the way in which lines between "us" and "them" are being drawn in our understandings of the relationship between individuality and community.

"Kian's Diary": Kian of Westlife as the (Ironic) Ideal Ego of the Celtic Tiger

In a classic work of media content analysis, Adorno examines astrological columns in the *New York Times* in order to illustrate how astrology serves a variety of ideological functions in American society. Adorno's (1994) critique of astrology focuses on how it operates as wish fulfilment, exploiting ego weaknesses, narcissistic defences and other vulnerabilities of its readers in order to reproduce the dependence of individuals on its advice. Specifically, astrological advice is positioned midway between the actual social location of the reader, and that of their ego ideal — how they ideally imagine themselves. The point of Adorno's analysis is to demonstrate how astrology, like the American culture industry as a whole, is complicit in reproducing the ideological illusion that individuality can be achieved through consumption, and thus reproduces dependent, authoritarian personalities wedded to an ethic of consumerism. Although his analysis of the culture industry has been critiqued for posing consumers of culture as uncritical, passive "cultural dupes", in contrast to our current understanding of readers/viewers as active and critical agents in the consumption of culture, his notion of culture as wish fulfilment and his use of psychoanalysis in formulating the collective unconscious of American consumerism provide an interesting angle on our understanding of contemporary Irish culture.

Using Adorno's analytic model, we will demonstrate how Irish ambivalence to individualism is manifest in the ideological representation of the superiority of the local over the global in Kian from Westlife's weekly column in the *RTÉ Guide*. Although most readers probably read this column ironically or with tongue in cheek, and aware that the portrayal of Kian in this column is a fantasy construction concocted in combination with his publicist and an *RTÉ Guide* writer, this particular construction of Kian operates as the ego-ideal of how we should negotiate the excesses of globalisation that the Celtic Tiger has brought: he is at home in the global, yet espousing the values of the local. Despite its "over the top" quality, this column is appealing in that we are allowed to flesh out our new self-perception, our collective fantasy of our imagined, new cosmopolitan selves through vicariously experiencing the fame, glamour and travel of the band Westlife. Thus Kian, and similar new Irish "celebrities" become "ideal types of the new dependent average" (Adorno and Horkheimer, 1992). In this column, Kian, a lad from Sligo, is portrayed as hard-working, self-denying, able to have a few pints but not get carried away with the glitz, glamour and excess of the international jet set. Thus Kian has internalised the panoptic gaze of post-Catholic Ireland in not succumbing to sexual, pharmaceutical or material excesses that often accompany wealth and fame. Kian is portrayed as a "good boy" who "misses his mammy". For instance, most columns start or end with a statement of how little sleep he's had, "I got up at 6.00 am to write this" which represent him as committed to the folks back home despite his busy schedule. Kian writes home every week, no matter how tired, thus portraying the new Irish global elite as self-sacrificing ambassadors for Ireland and continuing the tradition of the loyal emigrant. Like generations of Irish emigrants, he is hard-working and also hard-playing, and even his play is a form of work: he jet sets at parties with the likes of Lionel Ritchie, George Michael, Mariah Carey, yet implies that these parties are for the good of Ireland, to illustrate the basic decency of Irish people to the global stage. As well, the portrayal of Kian is intended to illustrate the superiority of Irish values over more international ones: he relocalises the global by describing these parties as "a good laugh", "a great buzz" or "good craic", yet a pale substitute for "watching the *Late Late Show*, going to the pub with my friends", and when on tour he says that he misses Irish sausages, claiming the food on tour is "different" and thus inferior. Thus the phantasmic depiction of Kian as familiar with the global, but more fond of the local, as friends with the stars, but a good Irish lad at heart, is rhetorically designed to prematurely reconcile the contradictions between local and global by pretending that the global can be negotiated through the adherence to the values of the local; through the values of family, work, community, friendship and so on.

Similarly, in a separate article in the *RTÉ Guide*, Nicky from Westlife, one of the two lads in the band from Dublin, tells us how he writes to his girlfriend (incidentally Taoiseach, Bertie Ahern's daughter, and now Nicky's wife) "who's always been there for him, through thick and thin" reiterating and reconstituting the traditional Irish form of the chaste and faithful Irish couple, the boy away and the girl at home, the secular, lay approximation for the Irish person of living up to their ideal-ego, the Priest and the Nun.

The subtlety of this ideological fantasy woven around Kian and Nicky is a credit to the ingenuity of Irish boy-band impresario extraordinaire, Louis Walsh. Walsh is from Kiltimagh, County Mayo, which, pronounced "kulchamach" abbreviated to Kulcha, and then to "culchie", became the derogatory Dublin slang term meaning a bumpkin or peasant.

Walsh is a master at negotiating the delicate and fragile liminal spaces between the symbolic orders of community and society, the rural and the urban, the local and the global, tradition and modernity. As impresario, manager, and master of ceremonies, he knows the dangers of working in this liminal space. After their brief but intense experience on the global stage, Boyzone members are transformed, "shop-soiled" and "past their sell-by date". The encounter with the global transforms the clean-cut image of nice Irish boys to young men who are, if not corrupted by the world, then at least become too worldly. Walsh has reportedly ordered Westlife's Kian not to associate with a former Boyzone member, lest he be seduced by the dark side too soon, before his commercial potential is fully realised and exploited.

Though readers probably read "Kian's Diary" as a deliberate and self-conscious fantasy construction, this representation of Kian resonates with and expresses the desires of the contemporary affluent Irish: to able so speak within the vernacular of the local, and espouse cherished values of community, friendship family and hard work, yet be equally at home in the global, and an object of desire on the international stage.

Westlife's music exemplifies the absolutely "globalised" nature of Irish culture, in the sense that its blandness is completely non-specific in terms of place. There is nothing "Irish" about it, and yet this is, in today's terms, an exact description of what it means "to be Irish". In some ways, Louis Walsh's various creations add up to an attempt to create a new "modern" Irishness that is free of all tradition, all roots (and generally all energy), a purely surface Irishness, music as simulacrum.

Capitalising on the Localisation of the Global and the Globalisation of the Local

In this interchange or dialectic between the global and the local we get two apparently contradictory tendencies; on one hand, we have the localisation of the global, for instance when globally successful products in terms of format and structure, such as game shows, soap operas, are "domesticated" or infused with particularly local content. Global media corporations such as Sky, CNN, etc., dominate the commercial context within which RTÉ and the *RTÉ Guide* operate, corporations whose resources dwarf those of the local station. The success of RTÉ, its commercial survival and expansion in this context is remarkable, and is due to its keen awareness of the diversity of the market, but also to its capacity to effectively localise the global. For instance, RTÉ's success is due in part to its adherence to the local (its Irish content), but equally to its successful articulation of the local and the global, wherein the global — represented by Hollywood stars, world news, "blockbusters" and global American TV — is "domesticated" by the management practices of programming and scheduling by which global American TV is articulated with home-produced materials so that the local content of Irish popular culture is "carried" by global mass culture. An RTÉ audience watches the main evening news, in more or less equal parts national/local coverage, plus global news from CNN, Reuters, or an international news agency, preceded or followed by an American sitcom such as *The Simpsons* or *Friends*, and a major movie from Warner or Universal, interspersed with local products such as *Ear to the Ground* and *Questions and Answers*. In many cases, RTÉ's most popular products are "local" versions of global TV shows — *Fair City* as a simulacrum of *Coronation Street* and *Eastenders*, and, even more clearly, Irish versions of shows such as *Who Wants to be a Millionaire?* What sustains these shows is not simply that they are copies of the globally successful product in terms of format and structure — that is, their *formal* qualities (features that are generalised and universal) — but by their continuity of *local content*. Participants in quiz shows, for example, are asked questions from a field of global "general knowledge" or from the domains of global geography, physics, world history or international politics, in a form identical to that which participants in the UK or the US would, but they are also required to have mastery of the specifically local — the GAA, national history and Irish current affairs. The talent show *EuroStar* seeks to select a performer for the global audience of the Eurovision song contest, but the Euro Star is first and foremost a local hero. A large number of family and friends of the participants are in the audience cheering them on; the parish or the village from which the contestants come are "all behind them", "backing them", as though their moment of elevation as celebrities, as individual prize-winners, was in fact simultaneously a celebration of an entire local community.

On the other hand, we get the globalisation of the local, where, for instance, Irish writers such as Maeve Binchy take specifically Irish archetypes and values and place them in international contexts. What is mistakenly celebrated today as Irish "culture" is at times a massified Irish-flavoured product that promotes a homogenised version of ourselves for global consumption, but also for ourselves, in order to obscure some of the schisms recent and rapid social transformation has produced. In a similar way as the *RTÉ Guide* negotiates between the global and the local to develop its niche market, celebrity Irish "writers" like Maeve Binchy, Marian Keyes and Roddy Doyle owe their mass commercial success to adherence to the formula of globalising the local. Some of Binchy's stories, like those of Keyes, are set in modern, global, urban, rationalised and individuated spaces — Dublin, London, New York, Los Angeles; offices, apartments, airports, taxis, ferries; business trips, vacations, affairs and careers. Into these hypermodern and global social contexts Binchy reinscribes local and traditional archetypes and values — mothers, aunts, good friends, people who belong to families, neighbourhoods, villages, and communities; people who take care of one another, who rediscover and represent "real" values and "true" meanings. Binchy appeals to a globalised mass readership nostalgic and yearning for what they imagine to be, or to have been, and hopefully, perhaps still is in existence somewhere — in Ireland perhaps! — a more "authentic" form of life, peopled with "real" people who experience "authentic" emotions: reputedly she "writes from the heart" (*Plain Dealer*, Cleveland); she is "generous with laughter, generous with tears" (*Dallas Morning News*); "Binchy's warmth and sympathy render the daily struggles of ordinary people heroic" (*San Francisco Chronicle*); she "create[s] real people, touch[es] real emotions (*Chicago Tribune*).[1] That her stories are in fact formulaic, but are nonetheless taken for "real", is symptomatic of the enormity of what is lacking in global culture. According to Lacan (1994) what lacks is in *béance*; it "calls out" for help, for some-

---

[1] Reviews of Binchy's work in the foreword to her collection of short stories *The Lilac Bus*.

thing, anything at all that might help to fill the void. Irish pulp fiction provides this.

In short, the nostalgic American construction of Ireland as the locus of community, identity and authenticity that the popularity of Binchy's work reveals is a symptom of the "transcendental homelessness" that is considered to be a symptom of postmodernity/globalisation: of the fragmentation of community, the loss of identity, and the loss of sense of history. Transcendental homelessness "calls out" for the warmth of the local community —"Binchy is the next best thing to curling up in a cosy chair beside a cheerful fireplace" (*Illinois Times*). But the community spirits of the local that Binchy's necromancy calls back are empty husks of the living dead, representatives of what Beck has called "zombie institutions", old forms of social life that are already "dead", though we haven't yet come to terms with their passing. Though a much-loved writer who has been a source of inspiration to many Irish writers and talents, from this point of view Binchy's writing does a disservice to both forms of life, global and local, modern and traditional. On the one hand, her writing represents a conservative, reactionary moral stance to global culture: the conventional disavowal of urban, cosmopolitan forms of life, a refusal to acknowledge moral ambiguity. Her depictions and characterisations of the global, modern and urban express an unsophisticated and anti-intellectual inability and unwillingness to empathise with and to articulate the heroism proper to living in such post-traditional, de-localised contexts.

But not only are Binchy's global contexts and characters somewhat archaic clichés, her local heroes are as well: the fussy Dublin housewife, country girls who are innocent, but a little bit worldly too; the wise auntie who can give lessons in life and love to the career girl; handsome rakes, honest-to-goodness "sensible" types with "real" down-to-earth attitudes. Binchy is the "mistress of the innocuous"; romance without sex, without all that the fraught universe of human sexuality stands for in modern literature, from Baudelaire to Joyce to Garcia-Marquez, from Emily Brontë to Margaret Atwood and Toni Morrison; namely, power, conflict, resistance and subversion, the heroic struggle of ordinary modern people for transcendence, wholeness and the realisation of the Utopian potentials of the creative principle of Eros. In Binchy's writing, the vital energies of modernism are sent off to bed with a nice cup of cocoa.

Conclusion: Towards a Principled Relationship to the Globalisation of the Local/Localisation of the Global

In the cases above, we can see the ambiguous ways in which the emerging institutions of Irish culture and identity cope with problems posed by collision culture, that is, through the reconstitution of elements of mechanical solidarity within otherwise increasingly highly differentiated and individuated contexts to counteract tendencies towards egoism and anomie. The form and content of Irish celebrity constitutes an index within which we can see the tensions between individual and community, tradition and modernity, the global and the local. These tensions are not reconciled into one or another side of these analytic dichotomies, but rather are hybrid fusions of contrasting forms reflecting the liminal context of Ireland's collision culture. The "success stories" of contemporary Ireland, such as culture industry entrepreneur

Louis Walsh and pulp-fiction authors like Maeve Binchy are case studies in the negotiation of the liminal spaces of the localisation of the global and globalisation of the local.

These are, of course, selective "successes"; U2 is an example which occupies a somewhat different space — and one that is even higher on the global scale of "celebrity". Right now, U2, and Bono in particular, are probably the only Irish examples of the sort of celebrity who could enter the "pantheon" occupied by Elvis, Marilyn, Madonna, etc. And they are fully conscious players in the celebrity game, as evidenced by their Zoo TV and Popmart tours, and their manipulation of the media over the last decade or two.

As we have shown, the notion of "the Irish celebrity" captures interesting tensions between the tendency towards individuation and community, and between the local and the global. Our distinction between categories of the localisation of the global (as illustrated by *Fair City* and *Who Wants to be a Millionaire?*) and the globalisation of the local (as illustrated by the writings of Binchy) are in reality an analytic one, for both examples are only slightly different variations of the same process: the way in which through the process of globalisation, media forms become standardised and homogenised in order to reach a mass audience. The point we want to make in creating these analytic distinctions is the way in which the contradictions between the global and local get prematurely reconciled in popular culture and become subsumed by the imperative of commercial success.

From this point of view, one needs to look at not just what is said in the Irish discourse on celebrity, but what is not said, what is left unsaid. Perhaps the *RTÉ Guide's* condemnation of Hollywood stars is not simply local ethnocentrism, but in a sense an implicit repudiation of the problematic equation of commercial success with critical success, of the reduction of value such that "excellent sales" is the only measure of excellence. In the context of the popular celebration of the success of Ireland's "going global", what the *RTÉ Guide*, and more generally the ambivalent discourse on celebrity in Ireland keeps alive is the idea that "success" in contemporary Irish culture should not be measured solely by mass commercial standards, by the universal global standard of cash value. Historically, Ireland's strong tradition of literary and cultural excellence has never been measured simply by mass-market appeal. Ireland's unique contribution to modern global culture — Joyce, O'Brien, Beckett, Heaney and U2 — is owed to these authors' self-reflexive contemplation of the particularity of local experience in the context of the general and global experiences of modernisation and modernity, and of grasping and expressing the resonance between the local and the global in a manner that illuminates the moral practical dilemmas and ideals of modern people whose existence is always, simultaneously, both global and local. What needs to be kept alive in Irish cultural production today is the self-awareness that to succeed at globalisation is not simply to replicate its formulas of celebrity, quantity, and money value, which are ultimately fleeting and empty. Cultural success ought to be measured instead by standards that are deeper and that make a lasting contribution to the collective global cultural heritage. The question is: will the culture industry as it currently exists on a global level allow what is uniquely particular to Ireland's rich cultural heritage to survive?

CHAPTER 5

Irish Consumerism as Collective Gift Relations

ACCORDING TO A SURVEY ON CONSUMER spending com-
missioned by Deloitte and Touche of seven EU countries
and the US, Irish Christmas spending outstripped all EU countries and even the US in 2001. The Irish spent on average
€567 on gifts alone, compared to the European average of
€446, and the US average of €561, and the Irish spent the
largest amount on Christmas as a whole. This survey esti-
mated that Irish Christmas spending totalled an average of
€1,389 per household, including food and drink (€280) clothes
(€263) and socialising (€285) as well as gifts (*Business Plus*, 11
December 2002). In the words of Brendan Jennings, head of
consumer business at Deloitte and Touche, "The proportion
of Europeans celebrating Christmas is dropping, although not
in Ireland . . . Irish consumers appear to be planning to use
Christmas to let off steam by spending significant amounts on
gifts, food, drink, and socialising". (Consistent with what some
may call national stereotypes, this survey also revealed that
the Spanish were quite confident about their long-term economic prospects, whereas those surveyed the UK and the

Netherlands were quite pessimistic; the Germans bought the most expensive gifts; the Dutch bought on average the cheapest gifts and the most for themselves, and the Germans and the Belgians bought the fewest number of gifts.)

Interestingly, this expenditure is despite the fact that the majority of Irish consumers surveyed admitted that the Irish economy was flat or in a recession (with 78 per cent holding this opinion), and felt that their own household economic situation would deteriorate or weaken over the next year. Many of the lower-income families go into debt from which they may never recover. For instance, the *Irish Examiner* reported "consumers face massive debts in spending spree hangover" (24 December 2002). Michael Culloty, spokesman for the Money Advice and Budgeting Service, claimed that "some families on low incomes run up debts around €2,500 and they are unable to pay ESB, Gas and phone bills in January". The MABS is a non-profit organisation that provides free advice for such individuals, and has been running for 11 years. According to Culloty, "January and February are our busiest times . . . people decide to splash out for Christmas and treat their children. They provide toys and designer clothes for their kids and they're faced with a huge debt at the beginning of the year." The Director of Consumer Affairs, Carmel Foley, urged Irish consumers not to overspend at Christmas, and not to "overuse credit, since there is €1,300 million outstanding of Irish credit cards, which is double the amount four years ago and interest rates on cards is 7 per cent higher than the EU average" (*Irish Examiner*, 24 December 2002). As the Centre for Retail Research in Britain reports, shoplifting rates in Ireland as in Britain reach a high at

Christmas time. However, Christmas spending was not simply high in 2002, but rather has steadily increasing over the past half decade; in 2001 spending was up 12 per cent from the previous (TCM archives, 26 December 2001). Clearly, this cultural onus on Christmas spending is at odds with many individuals' real spending power.

For the most part, the response of individuals to what the *Irish Examiner* (18 December 2001) has called "panic spending" at Christmas have been profoundly negative, and have been either to locate the problem in some external influence on Irish culture, or to denounce "consumerism" as a symptom of the decline of Irish culture. For example, an *Irish Times* survey, Christmas 2002, asked, "Has Christmas been spoiled by crass commercialism?" and received back numerous, but largely negative, responses. Many exhibited the "externalisation" response, attributing mass consumer spending to factors such as "the Americanisation of Ireland", "the introduction of the euro", etc. In a similar vein, a business poll taken by Budget 2002 which asked the question "who is to blame for the high cost of living?" showed that some blame "the euro", "9/11", and so on. Others invoked the "denunciation response", claiming that "greed is endemic in Irish society," "we live in a greed culture". In a related article, a journalist invoked the Hobbesian rhetoric of "war of all against all" in describing the shopping frenzy in the post-Christmas sales, claiming there is a "war on the streets as the sales commence . . . after the 48-hour Christmas ceasefire, hostilities have resumed between God and Mammon . . . shots were fired at 6.00 am as the first Grafton St shops opened". (*Irish Times*, 28 December 2001). Whether reacting to Christmas spending in terms of the "externalisation" response, or the "denunciation" response, the majority of journalistic and public responses to Christmas spending articulated this as a symptom of the decline of Irish values of community and family, and reflect a general belief that the eclipsing of such traditional values by consumerism is one of the "risks" of the recent growth experience in Ireland. A few responses involved a more self-reflexive (if cynical) taking of responsibility for this inflated pattern of consumption, as revealed in comments such as "Dunno, too busy shopping to give question any real consideration" . . . "Yes, absolutely! Now excuse me while I finish the old shopping" . . . "Sure, but who cares?" But for the most part, responses reveal the nascent fear that Irish values of community and family are being eroded by crass consumerism.

Many recent texts have emphasised the negative effects of the Irish growth experience in the past decade, and have accurately documented how this greater productivity has resulted in benefits for some, but has reinforced poverty and social exclusion for significant segments of the Irish population. This perspective is perhaps best represented by the collection of analyses of recent Irish political economy and social policy in the ESRI's (2000) *Bust to Boom? The Irish Experience of Growth and Inequality*. Contributors to this book have outlined in detail the Irish growth experience and its social consequences in terms of whether it has or has not meant a growth in wages relative to increasing productivity, and from this point of view have assessed changes as either positive (i.e. when the greater productivity has led to increased wage force participation) or negative (i.e. when they have reinforced poverty and patterns of social exclusion). The majority of sociological literature in

Ireland on the Celtic Tiger in this and other texts documents how the Irish growth experience has simultaneously produced both positive and negative economic effects, and thus has produced both continuity and change (O'Hearn, 1998). For instance, this period of growth has facilitated increased labour force participation for women, and has encouraged female entry in a number of occupations including managerial positions, but this growth has not reduced substantial wage gaps between men and women and deeply entrenched patterns of segregated labour within the workforce or the home (Fahey, Russell and Smyth, in ESRI, 2000). Similarly, other research has shown how there has been an overall increase in hourly wages in the 1987–97 period, but there has also been a widening of earnings dispersion, which means that this increase has favoured the top of the distribution rather than the bottom (Barrett, Fitzgerald and Nolan, in ESRI 2000). More significantly, when inequality of distribution of disposable income in Ireland is examined in an international context, it is revealed that despite its rapid growth, Ireland has an exceptionally high level of inequality compared to other OECD countries, second only to the US (Nolan and Maitre, 2000). This literature demonstrates, quite rightly, how growth has resulted in both growth in income levels as a whole and growth in income inequality, and demonstrates how increased rates of productivity in Ireland have not been accompanied by equitable forms of distribution; rather, they show how the Irish growth experience has reinforced economic inequality, specifically as measured by individual and familial wages and income.

However, there has been a curious silence around the issue of consumption, and inflated patterns of consumption are rarely examined in the academic or popular realm, except for this response of externalisation (i.e. "Americanisation") and denunciation (the intrusion of "greed culture" into Irish society), both of which are seen as connoting a decline of Irish values. As a result, we wish to address this absence. We are interested in understanding how these changes in patterns of consumption enlighten us as to how this growth experience has impacted on changes in national and individual character. The failure of the academy or the media to address this issue reveals the paradox and ambivalence in Irish culture towards consumption. Given the strong public and journalistic outcry in Ireland about this intrusion of "greed culture" into Irish society, why is there such a contradiction between what people are actually spending, and our condemnation of such over-inflated spending? Rather than simply condemning these inflated patterns of consumption by externalisation and denunciation, what we need is an analysis that attempts to understand the motivations behind them. In short, we need a phenomenological, rather than a naively critical approach to consumption, since at the moment this critical position cannot account for why so many claim that "rampant consumerism" is wrong, but do it anyway.

A clue to the answer perhaps lies in the response of a small group of people to the Christmas survey. Some of those surveyed argued that such spending was in our national interests since "encouraging Christmas spending will counteract the slowing down of the economy". This latter comment expresses a fundamental aspect of the persistence of traditional communitarianism in modern Irish consumerism: shopping is understood as not simply selfish individualism, or even familialism, but as communal and moral; as contributing to the well-being of the collective social body. The diversity of responses illustrates that frenzied gift-giving is a symptom of two contradictory moments in Irish society: on the one hand, resulting from the period of economic growth experienced in the last ten years in Ireland, which has increased spending power (at least for some); and on the other, the persistence of the traditional system of gifting in contemporary Ireland. This combination of acquisitive accumulation and generosity, of possessive individualism and collective commitment, coexist in contemporary Ireland.

Gift Exchange and Solidarity

How might we interpret the extravagance of Irish gift-giving, even at the cusp of economic recession? To do this, we have drawn on Marcel Mauss's (2002) anthropological analysis of economics as a total system of gift exchange, a system that is obligatory and reciprocal, and which functions primarily to institutionalise social solidarity. We will attempt to show the persistence of the "gift relation" in the practices of consumerism in contemporary Ireland, that what frequently appear to be the worst excesses of egoistic possessive individualism, show also the persistence of a residual communitarianism, our residual deep need for community and solidarity. In traditional cultures and in contexts of scarcity, extravagance is periodic and contained within spatial/ temporal and moral boundaries of reciprocal gift relations. Country people after a fair-day or on a holiday ought to be *flaithiúlach* — extravagant — and at weddings and funerals food and drink should be *go fluairseach* — plentiful, in excess — but this excess is to be understood in terms of wider cycles of scarcity, deprivation, obligatory reciprocation and continuity, in what Mauss identifies as a total system of gift exchange pertaining to social systems such as pre-modern Irish community. Thus, extravagant expenditure in the context of traditional community was a principled and morally sanctioned way of collectively disposing of what Bataille (1988) calls the "accursed share", the excess, "surplus enjoyment" that is generated by and that sustains all social life. When the cyclical economy is replaced by linear progressive accumulation, the excess of cash persists vestigially as a problem of disposal. Peillon (2000) has shown how contemporary Irish festivals and celebrations, like the Galway Arts Festival, the "St Patrick's Festival Weekend" and fireworks extravaganzas in Dublin, are simulacra, new festivals manufactured by the tourism industry, and that these festivals perform the function of blowing off and consuming the surplus generated by the boom.

Shopping, as the central ritual activity of modern consumer culture, tends to displace and replace everything else, but its idiomatic content continues to display the unique and peculiar characteristics of local identity. In contemporary Ireland, instead of or, more typically, as well as, going to Sunday mass, some families now go *en masse* to do the family shopping in the Shopping Centre, and to the DIY superstore/home improvement centre, which open on Sunday afternoons after mass. Extravagant expenditure on the home and on children is legitimated as morally justifiable within a traditional normative order, as it is not "selfish" but contributes actively to the material sustenance and reproduction of the traditional institutions of the home and family life. Extravagant expenditure on family groceries and home improvement materials are morally sanctioned; just as participation in Sunday mass accumulates God's grace, home improvement increases property values, mutually enhances "desirable residential" neighbourhoods and the family's good grace with the financial institutions. Irish families use the spaces of the mall and DIY superstore just as they use the parish church, as an occasion to socialise and to keep an eye on the state of one another's souls — what they are doing to their interiors.

Thus, the most fundamental function of shopping may be interpreted in terms not simply of individual monadic consumerism, nor shopping as a social activity with residual communitarian qualities — Irish mass consumerism as described earlier — but in terms of the more elementary and fundamental relations of the gift as described by Mauss. The rituals of family shopping and the excess that pertains to the practice — its tendency to increase exponentially, especially evident during boom periods — functions primarily to establish, maintain, and reproduce obligatory and reciprocal relations of social solidarity. The family consolidates as family through parents as "breadwinners and providers" taking care of children and providing for one another; and being seen by other families to be endeavoring to do so. Shopping therefore shores up and reinforces the collective representations of the traditional roles of "the good provider", the "good Irish mother" and the good of "traditional Irish family life" to which we are all beholden and which have constituted elements of the collective conscience in Ireland. Against this background we can see the importance of the gift relation in reconciling the practices of Irish consumerism with more traditional aspects of our collective representations. The primary anxiety is that in the new affluence Ireland is becoming "less generous". Our collective representation has been that we are a generous people, that we "give more" than other (often far better-off) people, that we give more per capita to events such as Live Aid and other highly visible global charity drives; that we give more in terms of emigrants' labour to the building of the prosperity of Britain and America. By giving, we are therefore entitled to receive more — subsidies from the EU, American investment, foreign tourism — who come here to see how friendly and generous we are with our hospitality. In short, our honour, wealth, and prestige is increased by the system of reciprocal and obligatory gift exchange in which we are involved. This is especially evident in "the way in which we vie with one another in our presents of thanks, banquets, and weddings, and in simple invitations. We still feel the need to *revancherien*" (Mauss, 2002: 8–9).

Mauss's analysis is also relevant when critiquing the extravagance of Irish spending as apparent in Christmas shopping. That Christmas shopping is said to be "out of control", however, again illustrates the extent to which spending is channelled into an activity that supports Mauss's point; through reciprocal gift-giving and exchange, we support and ritualistically celebrate family and community. As well, extravagance is sanctioned where expenditure on communions, confirmations and weddings is concerned, since weddings, especially, involve the affirmation of family in the eyes of the community, two values presumed to be central to Irish identity. The extravagant wedding and its associated rituals — the engagement party, the wedding shower, the invitations, the stag and hen parties, the ceremony, the honour roles of best man, bridesmaids, maids of honour, pages, ushers and so on, the reception, the toasts, the "afters", the gifts — are all about the reciprocal and obligatory gift exchanges that consolidate solidarities of families, in-laws, friendships and communities. The participants are honoured by their mutual recognition, by their demonstration of their mutual reproduction of collective representations of family, community, friendship, and strong forms of sociability and solidarity. As well, weddings are competitive — people strive to out-do one another in extravagance, to give their guests "the very best" on the expectation and assurance of obligatory reciprocity. The antagonistic competitive quality of this practice can go so far as the sumptuary destruction of accumulated wealth to outdo rivals, thereby constantly "bidding-up" the price of social solidarity; meaning that in order to "keep up" and "fit in", to be socially acceptable, people must spend more and more.

All of this Irish consumerism, however, far from indicating the devaluation of traditional values of community in Ireland, shows paradoxically how the traditional values of community remain central, and how, in the context of social changes that are perceived to be threatening or inimical to traditional values, can in fact lead to an increase on their premium: that extravagant expenditure is spent on shoring up values and social solidarities perceived as being "endangered". The collisions of traditional and modern, egoistic and communal elements in the contemporary extravagant Irish wedding are reflected in the aggressive defensiveness of the contemporary manifestations of the gift relation.

Property and the Possessor Principle

This is also evident in the real estate market, in the spectacular phenomenon of extravagant "monster houses". The contemporary "big house" is an expression of the persistence of what Lee (1989) has identified as the "possessor principle". The possessor principle, Lee argues, is "deeply rooted in social structure and historical experience". Its source is "The arbitrariness of relations between landlord and farmer, and between farmer and labourer, [which] fortified in the Irish the craving for security natural and normal in an uncertain world. This expressed itself most obviously in an obsessive attachment to land" (1989: 392). The persistence of the possessor principle is reflected today in the extraordinary emphasis on private home ownership in the Irish real estate market. The possessor principle, Lee shows, is historically and experientially grounded in economic insecurity. Desire for the "big house", typically (and not insignificantly) simulacra of nineteenth-century landlords' mansions, now for "ourselves alone", express our new-found security, but, equally, they are symptomatic of our persistent anxiety about security.

The "monster" house is an especially revealing symptom of the persistence of the past in the present, the fusion of traditional and modern cultural forms in contemporary Ireland. "Monster" is derived from *monstrere* (Latin) meaning a Divine portent or omen, or *montre* (French) meaning "to show", "to put on display". In the symbolic order and ritual practice of Catholicism, for example, the "monstrance" is the device in which the Sacred Host is displayed and shown to the faithful. Thus we can see how an interpretation and understanding of the monster house is not to be found by analysis in terms simply of rational utility — as though Irish homeowners were demonstrating "rational choice" in terms of political economy, but rather in terms of analysis of the more fundamental libidinal economy. The first and most obvious aspect of post-Catholic Irish culture and identity that the monster house displays is the material embodiment of our desire for the Divine substance: the Word made flesh as the Sacred Host is now money, materialised in bricks and mortar; the house becomes the sublime object of the ideology of commodity fetishism, as does the practice of the elaboration of the interior that the ritual and devotional practices of "home improvement" and DIY represents. Yet, in Benjamin's (1999) terms, we can clearly see the persistence of the Utopian desires essential to religious life.

On the one hand, the hyper-inflated housing market and the emergence of the monster home may illustrate emerging cultural forms of individuation and egoism in modern consumerism. On the other hand, the presentation and illumination of new houses — laid out on a manicured lawn as though on a tray; floodlit by night — indicate that to some extent they retain the quality of a gift; in the minds of those who own them, such a house is a gift both to one's family and to one's community. New houses are perceived by their owners, and indeed by others, as "a beautiful thing", "a fine house to look at", and in this sense the big house is given to others, for the edification of the community. They seek recognition, reciprocity, that the gift-giver will receive honour in return — recognition, status, self-esteem, that in the eyes of the community they will be seen to be "doing well", thus raising the standard of the community overall. The reciprocal and obligatory nature of the gift relation means that the next person to build in the community must return a gift at least equal to, and preferably greater than, the last gift exchanged; i.e. a house that is bigger, nicer, more lavishly decorated than its predecessor, adding to the property value and the status of the neighbourhood collectively, and new homemakers must take ever larger mortgages to participate in this potlatch system. Thus, the obligatory and reciprocal ritual practices of "keeping up with the Joneses" is the contemporary continuation of the gift relation, the elementary form of establishing and consolidating social solidarity, but its inherent antagonism, its inflationary competitiveness, can become inimical to the very solidarity that it seeks to constitute.

The Larger Framework

In Mauss's analysis of the gift relation, the total system of gift exchange unifying pre-modern communities may be eventually replaced by a total system of obligatory exchange relations in modern society. The fully developed modern welfare state drawn up by Titmuss (1971) would be an example of such a system, where in exchange for taxation and democratically legitimated power, the state apparatus would reciprocally distribute goods in the form of social security, education, health and welfare and so on. This is the fundamental principle underpinning the social contract of modern democracy, explicitly in the so-called "new deal" of the mid-twentieth century, wherein the individual was incorporated in the collective social body "from the cradle to the grave". In the case of modern Irish society, elements of the traditional system remained in place, and compensated for the fact that the modern total system was never fully implemented. Mothers, families, and communities, for example, cared for their sick, disabled, and elderly members, where services were chronically underprovided by the state. This role was also filled by voluntary bodies, charities and most especially (and now infamously) by religious institutions. At the present conjuncture, this arrangement is breaking down. The traditional total system is unravelling by processes of individuation, placing increasing demands on the state to provide more adequate services, services which families, communities and the voluntary sector can no longer provide. And the modern total system, always underdeveloped, and now suffering exponential demand, seeks to cut back expenditure on health and social welfare, to defer demand and to limit claims to greater resources.

Theorists of the welfare state and social policy, such as Offe (1982), have shown that in general this is the plight of the welfare state in late capitalism. The UK, Scandinavia, the EU, Canada and Australia all suffer the problem of being able neither to contract (as older traditional institutions comprising the voluntary sector are no longer there to fall back upon) nor expand (as this inflates fiscal and legitimation pressures on the state) and they respond in similar measures: by privatising services, thus reducing the state's exposure to legitimation deficits, and by legally deferring and limiting claims, thus reducing the state's exposure to fiscal deficits. But in Ireland, due to the extraordinary reliance that the modern welfare state has had on the vestiges of the traditional system of church and community, and the chronic fiscal difficulties of the state, the problem is accentuated and amplified. In contemporary Ireland, even those socially included, are in a sense "excluded" or under-included. The social-partnership arrangements, so crucial to sustaining economic growth, are based fundamentally on obligatory, reciprocal and progressively incremental gift relations, trading productivity in exchange for moderated wage increases, and more generally for the provision of such things as adequate health services, now regarded as not alone chronically, but acutely, inadequate. The persistence of the importance of the gift relation throughout Irish culture, represented by the success of the social partnerships, indicates the reproduction of a utopian desire and deep need for solidarity, even — and perhaps especially — when both traditional and modern total systems of gift exchange are relatively under-resourced.

But the principle of reciprocity at the heart of the social contract in Ireland is betrayed by the combination of, on the one hand, political corruption, and on the other, the perceived inadequacy of the goods received in return for social participation. This is further complicated by the fact that this "political corruption" was, as stated elsewhere and examined again below, seen as an important part of the gift relation of traditional Irish society. Thus, what was seen as acceptable, if covert, practice, is now frowned upon by the very society which previously closed its eyes to the "corruption". And this is the basis of Ireland's "compensation culture". Compensation culture seeks to extort "gifts" from a social body that it is felt "owes something" to its members: the state and public bodies in particular, are increasingly regarded by sections of the public as no longer worthy of our gifts of trust and legitimation, and increasingly we cynically orient towards them in terms of how we might extract "cash payouts" that we feel are somehow "due" to us.

The Tribunals highlight the continuity of the traditional gift relation in contemporary Irish society, and both its positive and negative qualities. The paradigmatic gift, a gift that initiated the Tribunals, was the "gift" of £1 million from businessman Ben Dunne to Taoiseach Charles J. Haughey. Precisely because of its fundamental and universal character in social relations, Mauss says, everyone knows that there is no such thing as a free gift. When the giving of the gift becomes known, the question immediately arises as to precisely what is being exchanged in return. O'Carroll (1987) has shown the gift relation underpinning clientelism and brokerage in Irish political culture, where "strokes" (favours) are performed by "cute hoors" (wily politicians and power brokers) in return for support, loyalty and political legitimation from "sneaking regarders" (political punters, who ambivalently disparage the questionable morality of the broker, while at the same time admiring his trickery and ability "to pull a fast one"). The Tribunals are in effect a systematic process of revealing the precise content of institutionalised gift relations in Irish political culture in the context of modernisation and economic growth. "Gifts", payments to politicians, are reciprocally exchanged for "favours", which translate back into wealth, power, and prestige for the parties to the exchange. The traditional system of gift exchange continues, but is amplified and extended in line with economic growth.

The Tribunals themselves are in fact an extension of the gift relation that they investigate. Now, in return for very generous and highly publicised payments to lawyers and administrators conducting the Tribunals, taxpayers are told they will receive in exchange "cleaner power". The Tribunals purportedly perform restorative sanctions on corrupt relations in Irish political life, and in exchange for public funds, the Tribunals will "set the house in order". However, Corcoran and White (2000) argue that because the Tribunals' terms of reference explicitly rule out prosecution, their effects in terms of reflexive modernisation and reform will be negligible. Moreover, because the institution of the gift relation is fundamental, and the reciprocal exchanges of power and legitimation are deeply institutionalised in Irish political culture, an abundance of money simply amplifying a long-standing traditional clientelist practice, it is likely that the effect of the Tribunals will simply inflate the price of favours, as the risk of exposure to political power brokers is increased. Developers pay more to politicians who risk more, and gift exchange practices become craftier and more devious. Corruption remains, but becomes more subtle.

From Gift to Theft

The corruption uncovered by the Tribunals points towards the ways in which we can see on a more general level how the gift relation underpinning social solidarity becomes poisoned. Gift exchange is replaced by theft and the basis of social cohesion is eroded. Under conditions of globalisation, the system of taxation and central revenue based on the nation state has undergone a fundamental readjustment. Economic globalisation has meant that transnational corporations can organise their activities such that manufacturing activity can take place in one location (where labour is cheap and environmental controls are lax, for example) locate their corporate headquarters and R&D in another, have their primary market in another, and pay taxes in yet another country. Nation states compete with one another for globally mobile foreign direct investment. This has been the keystone of Ireland's successful economic development strategy. Transnational corporations with manufacturing facilities and financial management offices in Ireland pay 12 per cent or less taxes on activities. In France, Germany, and other EU countries, the standard rate of corporate taxation is 30–40 per cent. A pattern of asymmetrical gift exchange thus becomes institutionalised. Tax breaks for global corporations are exchanged for jobs that are relatively highly taxed. Transfer of the tax burden from the corporate sector to the individual, by direct (income) and indirect ("stealth") taxes on consumers, represents a transfer of wealth from poor to rich. Such negative taxation is a form of "theft relation". This theft is experienced in terms of the individual taxpayer being "robbed" by the government, but in fact the theft relation is more fundamental and socially destructive.

Richard Titmuss (1971) the primary architect of the postwar social contract, extended Mauss's analysis to provide a philosophical (moral) and sociological (structural-functional) case for the national welfare state. His position at the London School of Economics is now held by Anthony Giddens, the foremost intellectual advisor to Tony Blair. The context has changed radically. In Titmuss's time, the revenue base on which the welfare state's redistributive function was predicated was national. The state was in control of levying taxes on economic activity within its national territory. In the present context of globalisation, economic activity is conducted in a global market, and the national revenue apparatus cannot control this activity (Beck, 2000: 4–5). The revenue base for its redistributive functions is sharply contracted. This is of course not unrelated to the ideological hegemony of economic neo-liberalism and individualism, which are inimical to political will-formation to either defend the national welfare state, or to extend it, let alone countenancing the development of a supra-national revenue and redistributive apparatus to correspond with the global economy (Mishra 1999). In the meantime, national revenue, the redistributive agency of the nation state, is systematically deprived of resources to fund public health, education, social security and housing, the gift relations of welfare that underpin the modern social contract. Whereas the gift relation increased solidarity, contemporary theft relations erode social cohesion, and increase the likelihood of endemic social conflict.

Conclusion

We have tried to show how, contrary to popular belief, the extravagance of Irish spending at Christmas, weddings, housing, etc. represents the persistence rather than the erosion of Irish values of community and family. However, this particular expression of these values is extremely problematic, since it ups the ante at a directly economic level, driving up prices in the housing market, making house ownership inaccessible to lower-income families, and more generally, for those who cannot afford such extravagant spending at Christmas and weddings, forcing consumers deeper into debt. Irish people are per capita amongst the most deeply indebted in the western world, as we borrow heavily to fund our participation in consumerist gift exchanges. The potlatch system of gifting is all too frequently viewed romantically, as expressing the laudable values of generosity and hospitality and the solidarity of community. From the perspective of anomic and individuated modern society, the ideal of community that the gift relation seems to represent can appear attractive. But Mauss is at pains to emphasise the competitive and self-destructive tendencies in reciprocal extravagant expenditure that the nostalgic gaze of modern society naively fails to see — or chooses not to see! So even though it represents a continuation of the values of tradition, family and community, the gift relation reinforces social exclusion and increases the polarisation between rich and poor in Irish society. Further, the persistence of the gift relation in Irish society paradoxically hides the need for a stronger and more equitable infrastructure of taxation and redistribution through health care and social welfare in which the needs of members of a modern society are taken care of. In the context of projected cutbacks to health, educational and welfare services, the voluntary sector, and the "community" will be called upon again to compensate for the failings of the social system by their generous gifts.

CHAPTER 6

Between the Mountaintop and the Marketplace: New Age Travellers, Lifestyle Politics and the Critique of Consumer Culture

I N CHAPTER 4 OF THIS BOOK, we claim that individuals in contemporary societies often experience a sense of fragmentation, a loss of a sense of identity and a discontinuity with the past, a condition which Fredrick Jameson calls the condition of postmodernity. One of the symptoms of this condition is what Lukacs (1971) calls "transcendental homelessness", a condition where identity is experienced as precarious, fragile and uncertain. While this sense of fragmentation, loss of identity and loss of historicity is in some specific contexts relevant to the experience of everyday life in Ireland, overall we argue that the dynamic tension or collisions between (post)modernity and tradition are a better way of understanding the Irish experience.

Despite the coexistence of modernity and tradition in Ireland, the Irish countryside has often been identified as the site of traditional, communitarian values, as a locus of authenticity, and has thus been an object of the "romantic gaze" by both urbanised Irish and non-Irish people. In a variety of ways, the Irish landscape has been commodified and sold to tourists through walking tours, photographs, and so on. In response to this, Ireland's tourist industry is to some degree complicit in this commodification process, and ambivalently cultivates a particular version of Ireland within the "tourist gaze", a process which has been referred to as the "McDisnification of the tourist industry" (Cronin and O'Connor, 2003: 9). This process more generally is evident not only in the deliberated commodification of landscapes, heritage centres and other tourists sites, but also in the cultivation of "stage authenticity" and the "commodification of craic" in Irish pubs. However, as commentators have noted, there are complex and varied relationships between locals and outsiders in rural Ireland, relationships which are not always captured by a simplistic dichotomy between tourist and local which represents tourists as active and locals as passive and victimised (Cronin and O'Connor, 2003).

The relationship between "outsiders" and "locals" has been the focus of concern in Irish society, and has at times been posed as a relationship of exploitation, and in a sense, a "cultural collision". For instance, recent responses to the influx of refugees and asylum-seekers is an example of this collision between the local and the global. From a different angle, responses to Brody (1973) and Scheper-Hughes's (1982) respective studies on small communities in Ireland illustrates the extent to which local residents can (justifiably, in some ways) experience outsiders' scrutiny (as tourists, "blow-ins" or academics) as a violation of privacy. Of particular interest to us, however, is the way in which Ireland has been settled by a variety of "blow-ins" who have migrated from urbanised contexts in Europe, North America, and elsewhere, some of whom perceive Ireland as a place of "recovery". What follows here is an analysis of a particular type of "blow-in", New Age Travellers, whom we interviewed in the period 1996–1999. Many of these New Age Travellers, particularly those who migrated to the countryside, perceived themselves as "refugees from modernity", as "in recovery" from a variety of collisions — specifically, collisions between their utopian ideals and the reality of their lives in urbanised, fragmented or "postmodern" urban contexts. As is apparent in the following analysis, Ireland is perceived by many New Age Travellers as a respite or sanctuary from such collisions, as a place "outside" modernity, a perception which illustrates a particular moment of the construction of Ireland in the global imaginary as a place "outside" modernity.

In this research on New Age Travellers in Crosshaven, Cork city, the Beara Peninsula, and Dunmanway, we tried to determine how these communities could be perceived as symptoms of the crisis of community, and the crisis of meaning that some theorists claim characterise contemporary society. Because of its reputation in New Age Traveller circles as a desirable destination, we focused particularly on the community in Cool Mountain in the Bantry/Dunmanway area in order to see precisely how this community negotiated this tension between unity and difference, between shared common values and internal diversity that theorists such as Iris Marion Young claim characterise contemporary communities.

Like other communities, the Cool Mountain community was characterised by internal divisions, conflicts and antagonisms, largely focused around the issue of how to synchronise individual conduct and collective welfare. This conflict expressed itself in the formation of three different geographically distinct divisions within this community based on different opinions regarding what constituted an alternative lifestyle. First, the self-proclaimed "bogfield" community located several kilometres away from the mountain, which was where new initiates began their experience as travellers. Second, the foot of the mountain, where initiates could settle if they "graduated" from the initiate community and established their credentials to those on the mountain. If accepted by the community, they then had the option of moving up towards the top of the mountain to what appeared to be a more "communitarian" group. The differential ethics of these three grades were expressed in a different type of housing: the bogfielders lived mostly in caravans and were more mobile and temporary; the foot-of-the-mountainers were much more sparse, eclectic, and functional in their choice of habitat, living in rusty lean-tos, caves, wigwams, abandoned vans and self-made shacks; and the mountain-siders whose elaborate gardens, greenhouses, windmills, manicured sod roofs marked them as more overtly and conventionally "green". Despite their shared commitment to a particular lifestyle, this community is very diverse. Thus, the New Age Traveller community is an expression of these tendencies between diversity and identity evident in local, national and global experiences of community today, and as such can be seen as a microcosm of these tendencies.

As well, these three distinct groups exhibited varying degrees of commitment to a collectivist ethos and an ideal of community involvement that characterises conventional politics of the left. In terms of their relationship to a community

ethos, the more transient bogfielders were relatively periph-
eral to the Cool Mountain community, since most bogfielders
either went back to where they came from, left Cool Mountain to live in other New Age Traveller caravan sites, or began their ascent, so to speak, up the mountain as members of
the more permanent community. As such, the name New
Age Traveller is a misnomer, since it only really applies to the
transient bogfielders. In contrast, the mountain community
call themselves "settlers", perhaps revealing a utopian desire
to break ground on a "new frontier". Of the more permanent mountain community, several community members who
tended to live near the top of the mountain worked ardu-
ously at organising community projects such as the running of
the community centre and restaurant, youth groups, various
art, craft and educational classes, and supply runs, often can-
vassing the others to elicit volunteers.

Others, who tended to live near the bottom of the
mountain by the side of the road, experienced these attempts
as overly totalitarian, an infringement on the autonomy they
were trying valiantly to maintain, and thus, as an uncomfort-
able reminder of the over-regulated life they had hoped to
leave behind. Thus, the strongest division amongst the "settlers" came from tension between the communitarians and
the more libertarian mountaineers, which expressed itself in a
mutual antagonism regarding their respective versions of
community — the communitarians felt that the libertarians
were apathetic and not appropriately civic-minded, and the
libertarians felt that the communitarians were imposing unnecessary conventions and, thus, merely paying lip-service to
getting away from suburban values of conformity.

However, despite these ideological and geographically observable differences, what bound these somewhat disparate communities together, what the New Age Travellers sought in the Cool Mountain lifestyle, was the freedom to pursue their own life in conditions of their own choosing. The theme of recovery often recurred in our discussions with this community. Although some of the Travellers we met were German, Dutch, French, Spanish or American, most of them were English, self-proclaimed refugees from post-Thatcher Britain, and perceived the possibilities for self-determination as much greater living in a lean-to on the side of a mountain in Ireland than in a council flat in Britain.

Others chose life on the mountain to find a quiet space to "recover" from city life, having suffered some sort of personal crisis, trauma or assault prior to moving to Cool Mountain. As such, they can be seen as victims of collisions. Furthermore, they were quick to dismiss the idea they were engaged in some pursuit of the "common" good, or "higher purpose" and were cynical regarding the notion of an "alternative" lifestyle, claiming, "we are all just getting on with it really". Thus, most exhibited a scepticism towards the possibilities of community in effecting some sort of social change or transformation in the broader society. Thus, what was expressed was not so much the desire for the recovery of some sort of agrarian idyllic, mythical past, a mechanical solidarity, a close-knit community, but rather the recovery of some sort of agency, the right to self-determination that they felt had been eroded through the combined effects of the dismantling of the welfare state, the introduction of the public order acts in Britain and the excesses of modern life. In a sense, they were refugees from modernity, casualties of the collision between their desire for the personal freedoms which characterise modern cosmopolitan existence and the reality of their lives.

This New Age community also expressed a strong ambivalence towards their retreat to the mountain. Most made no claims to seeing themselves as gurus or role models for how to organise an alternative community, or made any pretence of moral superiority. Unlike Nietzsche's (1986) prophet Zarathustra, who advises his friend to flee up the mountain into solitude to escape the "poisonous flies" and the "solemn buffoons" of the marketplace, these mountain dwellers did not feel antagonistic towards or superior to the local farmers and members of the surrounding community. Despite their desire for solitude, they were not separatist in orientation. Most were friendly, if non-committal to us when conducting our research, several had children in the local school, and most had amicable, if minimal relations with local farmers. Neither did they imagine that their mountain-dwelling solitude was preparing them to be prophets of the people or philosopher kings. Rather, several were self-mocking, quick to condemn their "escapism" from "reality", and felt torn between the life they had carved out for themselves on the mountain and the lives they had left behind, ambivalent about staying, ambivalent about returning. In a sense, they were caught between their previous homes and the mountain, between two worlds, and were aware that their "escape" was only illusory, temporary, and that there is really no refuge, no utopia, no place outside the social, outside of the complexity and fragmentation of modernity in which to heal.

While many New Age Travellers had very good relationships with members of the local community, some were criticised by the broader community for their lack of participation in the formal economy. In our experience, New Age Travellers have at times been characterised as "parasites" and "freeloaders", as "wasters" and "knackers". This anxiety expresses a legitimate concern that the already overstretched welfare state cannot withstand more strain. However, the vehemence with which some of these negative sentiments are expressed would indicate that New Age Travellers are sometimes feared and disliked not because of the potential drain on the welfare state, but because of the possibility that they will further destabilise traditional values already eroded by modernity. In a sense then, some of the critiques of their potential drain on the welfare state merely give a rational, economic veneer to a more generalised fear of difference, change and diversity.

From this point of view, Travellers are not necessarily consumptive, hedonistic, freeloaders "living off the dole", but rather have attempted to live off the waste of others, to establish a principled relationship to the global community, an awareness of the complex and abstract political economy of modernity in a broader sense. They have attempted to cultivate an environmental ethic at a more complex level than more abstract versions of New Age Environmentalism that focus on developing an environmental "consciousness". By living off the garbage heap, they are inverting the structure of modernity that would designate themselves as welfare recipients, as useless, unproductive, as waste products themselves.

In a sense, their choice to live long-term in temporary dwellings is a literal expression of this identity crisis, of what

Lukacs calls "transcendental homelessness", a condition of modernity whereby we want to recreate our origins, to rewrite or rediscover our roots, yet know this cannot be done. To Lukacs, this transcendental homelessness emerges out of the tenuousness of identity, the experience of identity as "kaleidoscopic and changeable", "nefarious and evasive", and hence is a symptom of the postmodern scepticism towards origin myths and scepticism towards the dissolution of grand narratives. In the words of Lukacs, we are both "secular, but yearning for the sacred, ironic, but yearning for the absolute, individualistic, but yearning for the wholeness of community, fragmented, but yearning for immanent totality" (Lukacs, 1971).

This ambivalence towards utopias, this appreciation of paradox, this tolerance of contradiction, was itself the basis of the production of meaning in the lives of the Cool Mountain residents. For example, they found humour in the discrepancy between the highly specialised, responsible positions many of them had previously held (engineer, teacher, computer scientist) and the mundane nature of their current struggle to stay dry, warm and fed. Several had self-consciously and ironically fashioned habitats for themselves that were emblems of those very aspects of modernity they were anxious to escape, and which were seriously at odds ideologically with the lifestyle they had produced: an old ambulance, a tourist information booth. To interpret this merely as an aesthetic gesture or as post-modern pastiche, however, is to miss the political economy of the travellers; for this recycling of the artefacts of modernity has a much more central significance to the traveller lifestyle than this.

However, subsisting purely on the waste of modernity was what gave New Age Traveller's lives meaning, what they prided themselves on, the focus of their creative and aesthetic sensibilities, their definition of skill, and what unified them as a community. Making the productive unproductive, the unusable usable, was the basis of their shared relationship to the environment and their role in the political economy of modernity. For example, they would diligently scour dumps for material for housing, clothes, furniture and anything that could be recycled, a practice they called "seagulling". Supermarket rubbish bins were routinely searched for bags of thrown-out food, although apparently some had taken up the practice of dying food unpalatable colours such as blue to discourage this practice. To New Agers, the challenge of mountain life is based on refining one's skill, regarding how to create a use value out of what is abandoned, thrown out. Who is designated an informal community leader is often dependent not on sociability, intelligence or other abstract values, but rather who is most accomplished at this process. As such, the New Age Travellers are not consumptive, hedonistic, freeloaders, "wasters", "living off" the dole, as they are sometimes characterised, but are attempting to establish a principled relationship to the global community and to the political economy of modernity.

Thus, the simultaneous unity and division within the New Age Traveller community in Ireland is illustrative of the tensions between difference and identity, between the need for the tolerance of heterogeneity, and the necessity for some common "unifying principle" that characterise the contemporary "crisis of community". These tensions have emerged historically from the process of social differentiation imposed by the increasing heterogeneity of modernity, the increasing fragmentation of the social along the lines of class, race, ethnicity, gender, and whole other ranges of "differences" currently under discussion in debates and struggles around the politics of representation. Feminists, postcolonialists and others have shown how unitary, essentialist versions of community can be experienced as totalitarian by voices from the margins. However, this politics of difference, this recognition of the heterogeneity of community, this sensitivity to voices from the margins has caused a crisis of community, insofar as in our scramble to accommodate difference, what binds us together, what constitutes us as a community at a neighbourhood, a local, or any other level of abstraction, is increasingly elusive. In short, we can no longer locate a notion of "the common good". As such, the challenge to contemporary communities, is, according to Hegel (1977), to "cancel the opposition but preserve the difference".

However, the New Age Traveller community *is* unified in its commitment to the possibility of some sort of utopian imaginary. These Travellers are unified in their shared experience of living the tension between the "is" and the "ought", experiencing the paradox of life midway between, in Nietzsche's words, the market and the mountaintop. The disparate factions of this community are not, however, unified in their capacity to successfully negotiate this tension. The bogfielders, as the most recent and traumatised refugees of post-Thatcher Britain, live perhaps a little too close to the marketplace, and are in a sense, "damaged goods". Their more frequent crises, their higher rate of substance abuse (or so it appeared from my discussions with a group of extremely friendly but troubled core bogfielders, who would often get themselves into a state of obvious intoxication on weekends in the local pubs) indicates they are still inextricably bound up in the excesses of modernity they hoped to escape. The mountain-toppers are perhaps a little intoxicated by the possibilities of reconstructing an alternative community in their own image, and perhaps it was a reflection of their own somewhat authoritarian tendencies that they chose to live on the top of the mountain.

The New Age Travellers are united in their search for meaning that Jameson (1991) and others claim characterises postmodernity. They attempt to preserve, in the face of overwhelming resistance, the utopian possibilities of some sort of ethical life based on a new relationship to the land, a broader notion of ecology, of the global community, than that which characterises the political economy of "normal life", or even a conventional environmental politics. The collapse of the range of utopian possibilities, however, to the refining of their skill at living off this waste, is perhaps indicative of the extent to which the realm of possibilities for the pursuit of an ethical life narrowed in contemporary life, to a postmodern "politics of the local". In the words of Hegel, "By the little that now satisfies the Spirit, we can measure the extent of its loss" (Hegel, 1977: 5).

Undoubtedly, the New Age movement's orientation to holistic health, self-help therapy and other "technologies of the self" do contain moments that are individualist, self-preoccupied, and which do espouse self-knowledge as an end in itself. This does not mean they are of the same order as the individualism of consumerism; for instance, such holistic medicines are usually "nature-based", and are therefore linked with environmentalism. Moreover, aspects of New Age environmentalism that advocate "green consumption" and more "environmentally friendly" forms of industry are most definitely positive developments. Nonetheless, the example of New Age Travellers, the less commodified end of the New Age spectrum, reveals to us that there are other ways of adopting an ethical position to the environment that in many ways transcend most of our capacities to think of how to deal with the environmental crisis. Although not all Travellers who are trying to reject the values of consumer society by living off the waste of others are strongly politicised, all of them have a general notion of the importance of reusing, re-cycling and re-invigorating these "dead" objects.

Although the New Age Travellers on Cool Mountain had a strong critique of capitalism and the state, their politics are much more consistent with the Foucaultian "micropolitics of resistance" than a more centralised and state-focused Marxist or Green model of political organisation. Nonetheless, we have tried to illustrate how this model is effective as well. What New Age Traveller life on Cool Mountain ascribes to is a version of human excellence or of virtue in a classical sense which values frugality over consumerism, control over con-sumption rather than the modern Protestant work ethic or yuppie ethics of consumerism, living off waste rather than producing it, and conservation rather than sanitation. More importantly, perhaps, this locates the realm of the political in everyday practices rather than simply large-scale political ac-tion: an attempt to live a unified life in the face of the inevita-ble fragmentation of the self which MacIntyre (1981) claims characterises modernity.

This unusual notion of virtue which characterises the New Age Traveller community on Cool Mountain is one attempt to live life as a unity, a whole, and to establish an ideal of "the good life" which preoccupies MacIntyre in *After Virtue*. As such, it is a response to what MacIntyre characterises as "the partitioning of human life into a variety of segments, each with its own norms and modes of behaviour" (MacIntyre, 1981: 190). It is an attempt to construct a moral community in the face of the moral incoherence of contemporary society which MacIntyre attributes to both the failure to recognise that contemporary moral theory is a series of disconnected fragments displaced from their original contexts (MacIntyre, *ibid*: 2), and to the moral vacuity of instrumental rationality.

In this way, this New Age Traveller lifestyle can be interpreted as a type of anti-consumer activism which challenges the intrusion of the commodity form into all avenues of public and private space. Some aspects of this anti-consumerism can be understood as subcultures of resistance to neo-liberal globalisation within the tradition of the Birmingham School of Cultural Studies. Hebdige (1979) illustrates how punks deliberately and purposefully crafted a strongly oppositional "style" of dress, jewellery, music, and general demeanour designed to expose the social contradictions of post-war Britain during the unemployment crisis of the 1970s and early 1980s. In his terms, the subversive power of punk lay in its power to wage "semiotic warfare", to provoke visual outrage that disrupts the taken-for-granted world, through, for instance, semiotically subverting authority figures and symbols such as the Queen, Thatcher, and the British flag. He says "the challenge to hegemony which subcultures represent is not issued

directly by them . . . rather; it is expressed obliquely in style
. . . the objections are lodged, the contradictions displayed . . .
at the profoundly superficial level of appearances" (Hebdige,
1979). Whereas punks expressed a "semiotic resistance" to
the post-war hegemony in Britain, New Age Travellers expressed a more generalised type of resistance to consumer
society, in engaging in a lifestyle politics resistance at a micro-
political level. However, as our analysis illustrates, the version
of the Irish countryside as a romantic escape from modernity
is increasingly becoming eroded by the forces of accelerated
modernisation, and are making it increasingly difficult to sustain this romantic ideal.

Since the time of our study, there have been dramatic
changes to this particular New Age Traveller community; the
land they lived on has since been reclaimed, and many members have been evicted. Nonetheless, the lifestyle politics of
these New Age Travellers can be seen as "micropolitics of
resistance" to consumer society, and a response to globalisation. As such, the fact that New Age Travellers find it increasingly hard to identify these places they perceive as "outside
modernity" illustrates how Ireland is in the throes of a variety
of collisions between "old" and "new" forms of cultural life.
The Irish countryside continues to be the object of the romantic gaze; however, the paradoxical forces we describe
throughout this book make this fantasy increasingly difficult
to sustain. Nonetheless, the anti-consumer sentiments expressed by this subculture have been mobilised at a global
level through anti-globalisation protests and movements in a
variety of contexts.

CHAPTER 7

What Was the "Celtic Tiger"? A Semantic Deconstruction of a Collective Representation

> Traditional Ireland worshipped its authorized self-portrait with an idolatrous fervour. . . . The portrait faded away. But no alternative self-portrait would emerge to command comparable conviction. . . . The more mature a people the less their need for a flattering self-portrait. It would be intriguing to think that the Irish have outgrown that phase (Lee, 1989: 652–3).

IN ORDER TO UNDERSTAND THE EFFECTS recent transforma-tions in Irish society have had on collective identity (and vice versa), it is important to understand the particular nu-ances of the term "Celtic Tiger". Though coined originally by a Dublin economist to refer to export-led economic boom fuelled by tax incentives to transnational corporations,[1] as

---

[1] A development strategy pioneered in Ireland in the 1960s with the insti-tutionalisation of the world's first tax-free manufacturing and export zone by Shannon Free Airport Development Company and copied throughout the world by national development agencies. This strategy, combined with local labour, cultural and market conditions, produced local and regional booms in certain Asian economies in the 1980s.

exemplified in the so-called "Asian Tiger" economies of south-east Asia — Malaysia, South Korea, and others — the "Celtic Tiger" quickly attained a diverse and ubiquitous usage, extending from the realm of political economy to encompass Irish culture and identity in general. During the economic boom of the mid- and late 1990s, the term "Celtic Tiger" enjoyed a wide usage in Irish culture, in both the discourses of the contemporary public sphere and the vernacular contexts of everyday conversation, sociability, and pub-talk. It was freely used in political rhetoric by the Taoiseach (Prime Minister), Minister for Finance, Government and Opposition spokespersons; its use was widespread in socio-economic commentary and analysis in the mass media, including in the business press, and amongst professional economists — the President of the Irish Stock Exchange, professional stockbrokers with transnational financial institutions — and academics; it had local, national, and global currency, and its use was ubiquitous throughout Irish popular culture.

The Celtic Tiger can be understood as what Durkheim (1995) calls a "collective representation". Collective life is constituted by the continuous portrayal of itself by its members, a portrait comprised of images and ideas expressed in "words, spoken and remembered: opinions, stories, eyewitness reports, legends, comments and hearsay" (Berger, 1985). The elementary shared images and ideas that make up the members' unfinished portrait of themselves are what Durkheim calls "collective representations". Society, according to Durkheim, is comprised entirely of collective representations, which are historically formed, re-formed, adapted and institutionalised, across time and space. They are "the product of an immense co-operation that extends not only through space but also through time; to make them, a multitude of different minds have associated, intermixed, and combined their ideas and feelings; long generations have accumulated their experience and knowledge. A very special intellectuality that is infinitely richer and more complex than that of the individual is distilled in them" (Durkheim, 1995: 15). Collective representations are the shared ideas according to which members of society make moral judgements as to what, for them, is the true, the beautiful, and the good, and on which they model action and practical life. A collective representation is a name for, a way of signifying, the values we share and the ideals we aspire towards; the desires, fears, anxieties and hopes that animate and motivate the social body, that inspire us. These collective ideas, the elementary forms of social life, are fundamental to each and every collective action and social practice: economic, political, moral and aesthetic. A collective representation is a shorthand form in which we find condensed the animating principles, the vitality of society, the collective *esprit de corps*, the *Zeitgeist*, the spirit that unifies and vivifies collective life in a given time and space. The Celtic Tiger is a collective representation that expresses the libidinal economy that underpins and animates the Irish political economy. It collects and represents the desires, conceits, fears and anxieties not just of the marketplace, but also of the social body as a whole.

Modern societies share in common with traditional communities the elementary forms of collective life. The fundamentals of collective life are religious, in the sense that "religion" — from *relige*, meaning "to bind together" — means to share collective representations, to have the same ideas as others. What unites us as members of distinct collectives is our shared agreement on, belief in, and usage of, collective representations. In primitive communities the content of collective representations are relatively clear, cohesive, undifferentiated and all-encompassing. In modern societies our mythologies are very numerous and highly differentiated, and the condensations and over-determination of meanings in our collective representations are more abstract and allusive. Durkheim gives the example of the flag in the symbolic order and imaginative structure of modern nationalism. Behind the "star spangled banner", the "union jack", or the national "tricolour", are marvellously complex histories and collective mythologies, that are nevertheless collected and represented by such mundane symbols as flags, which function as "sublime objects of ideology" (Zizek, 1989) that collect us as Americans, British or Irish. The "Celtic Tiger" is a striking example of a collective representation, an image in which are condensed elements of tradition and modernity, the global and the local, community and society, as they are in flux in the liminal contexts of collision culture.

A collective representation is a collective idea that represents how we see and understand ourselves, and how we express our self-understanding. And indeed a collective representation is not just something formed and shared by "ourselves alone".[2] It is also formed by the knowledge (always more or less partial and perspectival), the imaginings and

---

[2] "Ourselves alone" translates in Irish as Sinn Féin, the name of a radical Irish independence movement since the late nineteenth century, and the name of a nationalist party in Northern Ireland since the 1970s, the political wing of the Irish Republican Army.

fantasies that others have of us, and the reciprocal exchanges and combinations of these ideas. Central aspects of collective representations of Irish identity, the rich inheritance of cultural lenses and mirrors through which we see ourselves, are British (historically), and American (more recently) mainly, though there are many others, and thus collective representations are transcendent, independent entities, social facts, that do not necessarily correspond with empirical "reality" as perceived and construed by other discourses. Such is the status of the "facts" perceived and held to be known as "true" by ourselves, and by others, and such facts underpin and motivate action — by the Hungarian Foreign Minister, for example, when he says that Ireland is seen "as the main inspiration, model and image" that Hungary looks toward in "debates about how to preserve national identity in an integrating Europe and a globalising world".[3]

Furthermore, the economic boom that animates and is animated by the self-understanding expressed in the Celtic Tiger as a collective representation illustrates Durkheim's notion of a "social fact" (Durkheim, 1982). In the punishing conditions of the housing market we can see how the Celtic Tiger takes on the character of what Durkheim calls a "social fact"; an idea with objective existence that exerts moral force with material consequences. Its exteriority — that it is a collective phenomenon that transcends the individual sphere — is what gives it objective ontology; a social fact, Durkheim says, is a "thing". We know it is a social fact because it exerts a moral force, and has had economic or material outcomes that are very "real",

[3] Janos Martonyi, Hungarian Foreign Minister, Speech to the Institute of European Affairs, Dublin, *Irish Times*, 4 April 2001.

particularly for those who have been economically and socially marginalised. Under the collective moral force of the Celtic Tiger, people are pressurised into borrowing and buying. Banks and financial institutions automatically, and without it being requested, increase overdraft and credit limits; loans are "pre-approved". This pressure to spend is especially felt in the housing market, and if we resist the moral force, sanctions are imposed. We are financially punished for non-participation: we "fall behind"; we don't "move up the property ladder"; we don't "make the most of our investment opportunities"; we don't "establish a good credit history", thus "endangering future borrowing". The inflationary discourse of the housing market becomes a self-fulfilling prophecy — the material realisation of an idea, a collective representation.

The Celtic Tiger refers to the intangible and unquantifiable, but no less empirically real "consumer confidence" that ultimately underpins the economic actions of borrowing, spending, investment, speculation and consumption: the confidence — or nervousness — that is more usually designated by economists and stockbrokers in London, Tokyo and New York by the totemic animals of the "Bull" and the "Bear": the Bull, raging, charging aggressively forwards; the Bear, lugubrious, cautious, cantankerous, shying away, hibernating. Our totem, the Celtic Tiger, is a sign of our new strength and confidence. It is taboo to criticise the Celtic Tiger; to doubt his existence is a contemporary form of heresy, because economists (our Shamans) warn that if we undermine confidence in our totem he may abandon us or cease to be. As the "dot.com" bubble burst, politicians were careful not to use the "R" word, and warned us "not to talk ourselves into a recession". Thus

Ireland's Celtic Tiger is a collective representation of something as ephemeral and phantasmatic, but none the less absolutely vital, as "our belief in ourselves"; which is to say, more precisely, our belief in one another's belief in one another: our faith. This is morally binding, for to doubt, or to not participate, or to under-perform, is to "let the side down".

To say that the Celtic Tiger is a collective representation, a "social fact" with very real effects, does not imply that there is a unitary understanding of what the Celtic Tiger is, or that collective representations ever only have a singular interpretation. Rather, inherent in the notion of the collective representation is the idea that there may in fact be a wide diversity of interpretations as to what the particular phenomenon, in this case the Celtic Tiger, means. In all of this usage of the term "Celtic Tiger", what it is taken to represent remains unspecified, and yet the ubiquity of its circulation and currency indicates that its condensed and over-determined meanings are so widely shared that they can be taken for granted. This taken-for-grantedness of the meaning, despite over-determination and the diversity of individual representations (the fact that we may each have a different idea of what the Celtic Tiger actually refers to, and that this may change according to context) is, according to Durkheim, the *sine qua non* of a collective representation. That its meaning can be taken for granted as widely understood, that the Celtic Tiger has currency, shows that as well as being a transcendent symbolic entity, it is equally "live", "real" and "present". As a collective representation, the Celtic Tiger is a condensation of complex mythologies and is over-determined with many meanings, and to understand the animating forces of the form of collective life that it represents — contemporary Irish society — means that we have to systematically unpack its multiple and divergent significations.

To begin uncovering the diversity of representations contained in the notion of the Celtic Tiger, we should note that the Celtic Tiger is a compound of two distinct collective representations: the "Celtic" and the "Tiger", representations which, as we will demonstrate, are to a certain degree oxymoronic or contradictory. That it is the "Celtic" and not, for example, as it might be, the "Irish" Tiger, is significant. The idea represented by "Celtic" is resonant with pastness, with "History" writ large, but vaguely. "Celtic" connotes a remote, primordial history, a pre-national history, moreover, a history that transcends, and thus reconciles insular Irish history with the history of ancient peoples of the British Isles — Scots, Welsh, pre-Roman Britons, and the Celts of Continental Europe. The term "Celtic" invokes a romantic, spiritual, unified sense of history, rather than the concrete divisive historical "realities" of modern Ireland. "Celtic" represents a rejection of a sense of historicity that is nearby and "real" and expresses instead a desire to transcend history, to leave it behind, not by a leap forward, but by reaching backwards, to a time before history (modern Irish history at any rate) to a heroic age, a timeless time, a Celtic twilight that is also a perpetual dawn. The mist-shrouded Celtic twilight is the dawn of the Celtic Tiger because it represents a collective desire to "leave the past behind us", that past being the history of modern Ireland, colonialism in the nineteenth century (and its legacies throughout the twentieth century), nationalism and

Catholicism, and to repudiate their failures and their ethical practices of repressive self-sacrifice and asceticism.

"Celtic" is a primitivist representation, laden with positive attributes. Celts are "wild" and "free", "passionate", we live by our hearts. Thus, when reports show that the Irish are now the largest per capita drinkers in the world (that is, more than Russia and other deeply damaged societies), we are not seriously troubled by the news. It is easily incorporated into the collective representation of the Celtic Tiger. It is taken as showing that the Celts "know how to enjoy themselves", that we are exuberant and jovial, and global tourists come to Dublin not to see Irish "civilisation" represented by the city (museums, history, culture, as they might visit other world capitals) but to partake of Celtic "nature" — to "pub-crawl" — and to facilitate this in representations of Irish culture by the tourism industry, James Joyce and other modern Irish cultural heroes are reduced to a caricature of "the boozer".[4]

While the rest of the modern world is stressed out by the pace of globalisation, our inheritance as Celts enables us — or so we like to imagine — to "take it a bit easy", to keep our eye on what is "really important". This is how we see ourselves, and indeed how other globonauts see us; or more precisely, how we, and they, desire to see us: a Utopian Island of bounty and tranquillity in a stormy global sea of accelerated

---

[4] The place of drink in Irish identity is presently the subject of some anxiety and reflection. Is our drinking — like so much else — "out of control"? While not to deny the seriousness of the reality of Ireland's "drinking problem", it should be borne in mind that anxiety about our excesses recurs and coincides historically with periods of liminality — Temperance allied with Catholic Emancipation; again with Parnell, again after Independence, and again in the 1960s.

modernisation. Durkheim draws on the collective representation of the Celts as an archetypical traditional form of collective life to illustrate altruistic suicide: "a people lavish of their blood, eager to face death" (Durkheim, 1966: 218) who will willingly give their lives for the group. "Celtic" is a collective representation of a primordial Irish identity anchored in blood, race and soil. In an era of globalisation, transcendental homelessness, or permanent liminality, the collective representation "Celtic" expresses the desire for particularity; for authenticity in terms of pure racial lineage, desire to be native — "born and bred", or "born again" as Irish.

The usage of Celtic, of course, also expresses fear: fear of loss of particularity, of disconnection and dislocation, of rootlessness, of not mattering; alienation, anomie, permanent liminality; fear of the consequences of globalisation and accelerated modernisation. Twenty-five per cent of English people (and a similar proportion of North Americans) presently identify themselves as "having Irish blood"; while demographers say the percentage is in reality much lower. What the figure in fact represents is the desire of people in highly diversified, post-traditionalised societies with their own post-imperial and post-modern identity crises, to identify themselves with something perceived as being "more authentic", and thus by fantasy they find anchorage in something they imagine to be both transcendent and fundamental; and in the context of the fetishisation of the gene, that anchorage is provided by "race" — they have "Irish roots". The irony of course is that "race" is a collective representation, a social fact, not a biological fact.

In the collective representation of the Celtic Tiger, "Celtic" represents the idea of the good life as the life that is lived close to nature, traditional life as it is handed down from generation to generation, continuous life set against representations of modernity and modern life as fragmented, discontinuous, as un-whole and unholy. The "Celtic" in the Celtic Tiger is laden with connotations of sacredness and holiness, though not the modern Irish religiosity of Roman Catholicism, as presently this has become deeply problematical. The legacy of modern Irish Catholicism from the mid-nineteenth century to the present is now seen as — variously and cumulatively — tyrannical and oppressive, authoritarian, intolerant and xenophobic, hypocritically materialist, corrupt, decadent, sinful and immoral. Its moral monopoly is delegitimated and repudiated (Inglis, 1998). Thus, the religious life of modern Ireland can provide us with neither a sacred canopy nor the institutional infrastructure of values and principles that might guide us on the turbulent seas of globalisation and the temptations of affluence brought by accelerated modernisation. So again the inheritance we turn towards is the simulacrum of the religious life of a remote past, the early Christian Celtic Island (not even called Ireland then) the "Island of Saints and Scholars", or even more remotely the Pagan heroic Utopia of HyBrasil. As the new affluent Ireland of the Celtic Tiger throws out its old household gods, it needs to replace them, with simulacra of even older ones!

While the "Celtic" in the term "Celtic Tiger" conjures up a unified sense of history, and invokes notions of collectivity, tradition and continuity, the term "Tiger" resonates with a different, and in some ways opposite set of images, for the term "Tiger" refers to Ireland's economy and invokes the rhetoric of competitive individualism and its attendant ideology of survival of the fittest. This term implies a shift in Ireland towards a *laissez-faire* neo-liberal ideology (O'Hearn, 1998). As such, the term "Celtic Tiger" is oxymoronic, and the juxtaposition of the terms "Celtic" and "Tiger", with their respective and in some way oppositional commitments to notions of community and individual, history and economy, tradition and modernity, illustrate and echoes the ideological collisions going on in Ireland today. Firstly, the "Tiger" of the Celtic Tiger is intended to connote that Irish business is a force to be reckoned with in the global business area, for the Tiger is an animal that is ruthless, fast, powerful, a solitary predator which hunts, kills and is at the top of the food chain. Tigers command recognition and respect. It is a matter of national, collective, pride that "our" businessmen, like feral tomcats, "make their mark" in international markets.

Moreover, the fact that the economic boom is attributed to a Tiger rather than a Tigress is somewhat misleading, since a substantial proportion of the economic boom can be attributed to the entry of women as a "reserve army of labour" into the Irish labour force (O'Connor, 1999). The Tiger is represented as virile, erotic, luxurious, exotic, alluring, desirable and self-confident, all characteristics that we like to think of ourselves as sharing, characteristics which enhance the image of Ireland as an attractive and desirable place.

In his classic study of twentieth-century Irish politics and society, Lee (1989) analyses the collective representations that were formed and held sway in the emerging nation — Ireland as the beautiful maiden "Caitlín Ní hUallacháin" the embodied idealised form and romanticised countenance of "perfect *gemeinschaft*". "The self-image of 'traditional' Ireland",

Lee says, was ". . . characterised less by hypocrisy than by a capacity for self-deception on a heroic scale" (651–2). The same self-deception continues today. The Global Entrepreneurship Monitor of the London Business School, in a report on Ireland's business culture in 2000, notes that while there appears to be a consensus that Irish business enterprise is thriving, there is little evidence to support this. Ireland has recently enjoyed the highest economic growth rate in the EU, but it is at the bottom of entrepreneurship rankings. "With the notable exception of a handful of well-known entrepreneurs, Ireland has little entrepreneurial spirit, and is ill-prepared for innovation", according to the GEM. In a survey of 21 OECD countries, Ireland ranked worst overall in entrepreneurial activity. At the very height of the boom period in 1997, less than 1 per cent of the population were involved in starting a business, the lowest of the GEM international study. Of the new indigenous entrepreneurs, 86 per cent reported that they expected to employ fewer than five people in five years' time. According to Garavan et al (1997), some 98 per cent of Ireland's indigenous non-farm businesses are small, and are likely to remain small. Almost half of indigenous Irish companies employ between one and five people; 70 per cent have fewer than four employees; 85 per cent fewer than ten, and 97 per cent fewer than 50. If enterprises which employ only the owner are counted, then over 90 per cent of indigenous Irish enterprises employ fewer than ten people. Such small businesses have particular weaknesses and vulnerabilities. Frequent failure is due, for example, to "managerial incompetence and inexperience", "hiring and promotions on the basis of nepotism rather than qualification"; "inflated owner ego", "unclear business definition" and inconsistency, as owner-enterprises are not accountable to higher authority, as are paid managers.

The GEM study argues that all the evidence shows that economic growth is driven by enterprise, investment in research and development, and innovation. On all of these fronts, Ireland rates poorly by international comparison. The majority of Ireland's growth has been driven not by entrepreneurial activity, but by foreign direct investment. The extreme dependence of Ireland's prosperity on mobile global capital ought to be a cause of concern in the context of the rising cost of labour in Ireland and the expansion of the EU. There are some pockets of entrepreneurial activity, the much vaunted "software clusters", coaxed along by indulgent enterprise agencies, but this activity is geographically confined to Dublin, is new, and is vulnerable to global shifts. Far from being an international power, the Celtic Tiger, it seems, is a domestic pussy cat.

However, what the term "Tiger" illustrates is not so much a full-scale paradigm shift (in the Kuhnian (1962) sense) from communitarianism to competitive individualism, but its juxtaposition with the term Celtic illustrates tensions and schisms between the collective and the individual, the old and the new. The dual and contradictory connotations of the terms "Celtic" and "Tiger" illustrates the ambivalence of Irish people today who feel caught between what we at times experience as binary oppositions — the past and the future, the collective and the individual, the local and the global — whereby engaging with the latter appears to mean giving up the former of these "oppositions". As such, Irish collective identity currently resides in the liminal interspace between the discourses of the ancient, Celtic past, and the economy-driven future of the "Tiger". The term "Celtic Tiger" is the site of contradictory and complex meanings, a variety of discourses and interpretations, and is illustrative of the complexity of identity in Ireland today.

Despite its oxymoronic character, and the density of meanings and significations surrounding it, the term "Celtic Tiger" has become a utopian signifier of collective identity and vitality. Many cultural phenomena, sites and spaces, material cultural objects and celebrities are taken to be signs of our vitality, energy and identity; from urban renewal projects such as Dublin's Temple Bar to *Riverdance*, from Mary Robinson to U2. These phenomena are taken as embodying in some fashion the Celtic Tiger, a beast which has become the totemic animal of Ireland, a collective ego-ideal, a repository for what we hope the Celtic Tiger has become. According to Freud (1963) in *Totem and Taboo*, for primitive communities the totem functions as the symbolic representation of values and ideas, handed down, passed on by custom and tradition, and held in common by the members of community. For instance, the Bear, the Eagle, the Thunderbird are creatures that for aboriginal people embody idealised and/or feared attributes and qualities that distinguish and give particularity to their identity as members of tribes and peoples, and their stylised and abstractly represented forms, figurative expressions of their collective ego-ideals, constitute their totems. The Celtic Tiger can be interpreted as such a totemic animal. So for all the contemporaneity and modernity of Ireland's Celtic Tiger, its echoes and resonances are profoundly primitivist, traditionalist and communitarian. This enables us to understand the extent to which contemporary Irish culture and identity is underpinned by continuity with traditional culture and communitarian ideology. According to Freud, after the primal horde have killed the father, the totem represents the Father's law to which they are subject, their inherited tradition, the accumulated knowledge, ways of seeing and ways of doing, handed down by the ancestors and held in common by successive generations that constitute the members of the group as a collective body. In agreement with Durkheim (1995), Freud argues that when the totem is worshipped it is really the group's values and ideas, represented by the totem, that are being worshipped. The corollary of the totem as representative fetish of the group's values is the taboo, the prohibition and punitive repressive sanction against anything that desecrates, denigrates, or profanes the totem, thereby violating the group's values. Totem and taboo are two sides of the same coin, and thus our relations towards them are ambivalent. To doubt the Celtic Tiger, to dispute what are held to be manifest and self-evident truths of the "booming economy" and that "we are all doing so well now" is to risk showing bad faith and to be a heretic or infidel.

The disjunctures and ambiguities in the meanings of the Celtic Tiger have meant this term has been appropriated by a variety of discourses. For instance, the amalgamation of these terms and their respective connotations of community and prosperity has been strongly appropriated by the discourse of marketing, both within and outside Ireland, as a way of packaging authentic Irishness for both internal and global consumption. Increasingly, in the context of uncertainty and spiritual confusion, brand-name designer goods assume a quasi-religious function: consumers come to "rely upon" brand name commodities as icons. The consumption of designer commodities with high sign value provides a sense of continuity through recognition as belonging to a coterie of fashionable consumers. In a global era dominated by a trade in commodities with sign values by transnational corporations — Mercedes, Sony, Calvin Klein, institutions with resources of money and power as great or greater than nation states, — the "Celtic Tiger" becomes the "brand name" used in the promotion and marketing of "Ireland (Inc.)". As a representation, an image, a sign, the Celtic Tiger has a currency within Ireland as well as without. "Celtic Tiger Ireland" is the brand name of a commodity traded on global and local markets as a "location" for manufacturing and export, a "young, educated and flexible workforce", a "destination" for vacations, a sound and secure "investment", a "lifestyle" that is meaningful, moral, and enjoyable. The brand name is an image intimating and connoting the attributes contained in the collective representation, some accentuated, others underplayed. The articulation and rhetorical usage varies according to the strategic logics of local and geopolitical economy, and in this economy the "sign value" of Ireland is what is conveyed in the collective representation of the Celtic Tiger.

It has been documented how this notion of Irishness has been packaged and marketed internationally as a repository of tradition, community, authenticity (Slater, 2000), and how Ireland is perceived by North Americans and Europeans as a refuge from modernity. New Age Travellers, tourists and retirees from Germany, Britain and elsewhere come to Ireland in search of a more "authentic" life (Chapter 6). These global desires for "re-enchantment of the world" have been projected into the collective representation of the Celtic Tiger by the fantasies of a global Other who have lost touch with their own Gods. Paradigmatically, this is the American fantasy of Ireland, and global America's insatiable desire for God and fantastic projections of spirit onto Others (Celts, their own Native peoples) is why Baudrillard (1989) says that America is "the last remaining [or perhaps first amongst the new] primitive societies". The "spirit" of the Celts is imagined to "live on" in the cultural artefacts of contemporary Ireland, in the fetishised residue of the past: traces of folkways, language and idiom, music, and so on, much of it invented tradition, most of it modern, simulacra, copies of an original that perhaps never existed. The desire for this is so strong amongst others who desire for us to fulfil their fantasies of what we are, that people imagine that they see the Celtic spirit in the most mundane places. Guinness and Baileys are branded commodities that are fetishes: more than mere drinks, they are icons of Ireland, and through their consumption one imbibes, phantasmatically, the Celtic spirit. The marketing of spring waters, particularly Ballygowan, exemplifies this. *Riverdance*, for example, "brings tears of joy, tears of pride to the eyes of global audiences", "brings the world to their feet". For The Corrs, just an echo of a traditional air, a familiar refrain, "a fleck of culture" (Geertz, 1993) makes their meaningless ditty spiritual, meaningful, touched by the Celtic Gods. In these phenomena we can see how, as Hegel (1977: 5) put it, "By the little which now satisfies Spirit we can measure the extent of its loss".

The Celtic Tiger now marks the advent of conspicuous consumption as the basis of collective identity. Consumerism now vies with Catholicism and nationalism as organising discourses of Irish modernity, and as the basis of what constitutes "the good life". This shared belief — our collective, unifying faith — the power attributed to the Holy Spirit in traditional Irish religion/spirituality, is transposed into the symbolic order and imaginative structure of post-Catholic consumerist Ireland. The Holy Spirit — belief in belief itself — constitutes the community of believers that is whole and holy. As such a faithful community it is desirable, and stands opposed to the (undesirable) idea of a fragmented, individuated society (Peillon, 1984). The idea of community is consonant with Catholicism and resonant with nationalism and constituted the unifying communitarian ideology of collective life in Ireland for most of the twentieth century. The Celtic Tiger is the current post-Catholic, post-national — and insofar as Catholicism and nationalism have been the organising discourses of Irish modernity — post-modern, reformulated notation of this chain of equivalences and symbolic condensations: it is a collective representation of the idea of the unity and wholeness of collective life — the idea of the good life — in Ireland today.

As a collective representation of the good life, the ideological function of the Celtic Tiger is that it has sustained the "social partnership", successive "National Agreements" and "National Understandings", the corporatist social contracts of the "Partnership for Prosperity and Fairness" and "Sustaining Progress". This is the institutional framework within which ritual sacrifice (of wage claims) seeks to appease and win favour from the transnational gods of globalisation. The power of the Holy Spirit, represented now by the Celtic Tiger, is attested by the survival of the social partnership despite evil, sin and temptation; that is, despite stark class stratification (masked by the euphemism "social exclusion"), systematically institutionalised and normatively sanctioned tax evasion by a "golden circle" of the super-rich, and levels of use of public office for private gain typically associated with the nepotistic power elites of a feudal era, not with modern legal rational democracy. The ideological function of the "Celtic Tiger" is paradigmatically illustrated by the coverage by the Irish media of the purchase by Tony O'Reilly of an original Impressionist canvas at an international art auction during 1999. O'Reilly's purchase of the painting was lauded in the media (much of it owned by O'Reilly himself!) as an "Irish achievement" and a sign of "the wealth of Ireland", as though the work of art was an acquisition for the National Gallery, when in fact it was a private purchase for the exclusive pleasure of a global businessman.

However, we are profoundly ambivalent about the fact that the celebration of Irish affluence through conspicuous consumption (conspicuous to ourselves and one another) is the new cultural logic of Irish modernity. The divergent and contradictory connotations of the Celtic Tiger represent the ambivalence we feel towards our situation and ourselves. The paradox of modernisation is that with the emancipating effects such as cosmopolitanisation comes a more profound oppression, i.e. more deeply entrenched patterns of social exclusion. And in the same breath, as it were, we pay lip-service to the problems of inequality and social exclusion and speak of the presence of visible minorities as the bearers of our new cosmopolitanism who save us from our insularity, and whose coming here confirms our conceit that we have always been, and continue to be, a friendly, welcoming and desirable community. Those same others who we see as endangering our new society, paradoxically we feel are also constitutive of it. Those same others who erode and dissolve our way of life simultaneously affirm and reproduce it, reconciling local and global, community and society, past and future. Ambivalence towards immigrants reflects ambiguities arising from the paradoxical forms of life thrown up by dialectics of modernisation, the collision culture of contemporary Ireland. The ambivalence/uncertainty/anxiety represented in the Celtic Tiger as collective representation find articulation, expression and material manifestation both in the Irish political and libidinal economies: confidence and inflated expectations of the future that underpin investments, speculations, borrowings; and simultaneously anxiety, manifest in insurance, risk and the search for security.

The new significations of the Celtic Tiger as collective representation mark a transition: from a traditional and post-colonial society premised on communal values and a docile, dependent subject (the "quiet man" as the ideal-type subject of Church and Empire) to a modern society premised on Progress achieved by the self-determining entrepreneurial subject (the "self-made man" as a modern ideal-type). Much of the public discourse on the Celtic Tiger centres on judging the moral character of this transformation: *Is this change "good" or "bad"? Is the new Ireland the manifestation of our hopes and dreams, the realisation of what we have been striving for all along, or have we lost something good and precious,*

something "essentially Irish" that the new affluence cannot com-
pensate for? The liveliness and the blindness of this tautologi-
cal exchange of views derives from the mutually fascinated
gazes of the global and the local: the global Other (North
Americans and Continentals) look to Ireland in search of a
past to compensate for their transcendental homelessness
and loss of continuity, the existential conditions of modernity.
In Ireland, the global imagines it sees a community, it projects
a fantasy of a traditional Ireland that is spiritual, ancient and
holy.[5] Conversely the local (native, Irish) suffers the existential condition of being bound to place and time.

Churchill famously remarked that the difference between
Ireland and England is that the Irish cannot forget any history,
whereas the English cannot remember any, and in this he put
his finger not only on the crux of Anglo-Irish relations but on
what cleaves — binds together and separates — colony and
empire, local and global, tradition and modernity. While the
global looks to Ireland in search of a past, a community, the
Irish look to the global in search of a future, a cosmopolitan
society. There, in the imagined societies of globalised Continental and North American modernity, we project a fantasy
of a new Irish society that is modern, secular and materialist.

At the intersections of these gazes in theatres of collision
culture, we see through and glimpse the ruins of fantasies of
both past and future: as locals, we can see that we no longer
correspond with the idea that the global other has of us —
perhaps we never did! Nor do we want to correspond with

---

[5] A case in point is Edith Turner, *The Ancient and the Holy: the Root and
Flower of Irish Spirit Experience*, Virginia, University of Virginia Press (forth-
coming).

it, as it is no longer our ego ideal. And as globalised locals who have lived in New York and London, we have glimpsed the future, we have grasped the brass ring and sensed its turning to dust in our hands. In the global cities we see the image of "the iron cage of rationalised acquisitiveness convulsed with self-importance" (Weber, 1978) and we recoil from what we perceive to be the moral vacuity and atomised, high-stress lifestyles of global North American culture even as we strive to emulate it, as though we glimpse our monumental "achievements" our "progress" as ruins even before they have crumbled (Benjamin, 1999). All that is wrong with contemporary Irish culture and identity we blame on "Americanisation", yet the panacea for our ills is more accelerated modernisation. Thus we cleave nostalgically and defensively to our vanishing past even as we flee gladly from it. "Contemporary globalised Ireland", says O'Toole (1999), reviewing Seán Hillen's *Irelantis*, is "a society that became post-modern before it ever quite managed to be modern."

To say, as we do, when we reflect momentarily on the convulsions of our emerging culture, how "Ireland is a strange place" is to say, according to Marx, that Irish people are expressing our sense of alienation, our estrangement from our own culture and identity. Our alienation is threefold, Marx says. We are estranged from the product of our labour (we are drones in branch plants of transnational corporations, and "our" property is borrowed and mortgaged — on average over 60 per cent of Irish people's disposable income is spent servicing personal debt); we are estranged from one another (against whom we compete in educational, employment and housing markets); and we are estranged

from ourselves, our "species being" (as we become overspe-
cialised and overworked, our lives and our minds become
narrowly focused and one-dimensional). "The result is that
man feels that he is acting freely only in his most animal functions — eating, drinking and procreating, or at most in his
dwelling and adornment — while in his human functions he is
nothing more than an animal" (Marx, in McLellan, 1980). The
exuberant social phenomena of Celtic Tiger Ireland give expression to this alienation: as new-found affluence is insecure,
uncertain, alien to us, we construct and express our collective identity through animalistic activities of the tiger: drinking
and eating, and ravenous consumption; careless — usually
drunken — sexual promiscuity. Dublin has one of the fastest
growing rates of sexually transmitted diseases in Europe,
which epidemiologists link to Temple Bar's club culture su-
perimposed on a society infamous for its levels of sexual ignorance and naïveté. Much of what we take to be expressions of our new-found "independence" in the libidinal economy of contemporary Ireland are in fact artless and formless
expressions of under-sublimated and uncultivated animalistic
drives, symptoms of self-estrangement, not self-confidence.

We also experience a contradiction between the Celtic
Tiger's respective connotations of community and prosperity.
The deep-seated power of the Catholic Church in Ireland,
the source of its moral monopoly and legitimacy, is historically tied to material poverty and deprivation. "Religious suffering is at one and the same time the expression of real suffering and a protest against real suffering. Religion is the sigh
of the oppressed creature, the heart of a heartless world, and
the soul of soulless conditions. It is the opium of the people"

(Marx, in McLellan, 1980: 23). The new materialism creates the conditions for tearing down Catholicism and its Orders from their pedestals by providing an alternative god to worship (money); new altars, graven images and saints to patronise (commodity fetishes, designer labels); devotional practices and good works (pursuing one's career, home improvement); alternative rituals and pilgrimages (shopping, house-hunting, golfing in Marbella). These are new opiates that give us a sense of transcendence and relief from our new oppressions — not having enough work is replaced by our having too much to do; the melancholy of underdevelopment becomes the stress of accelerated modernisation.

The prosperous, vigorous, Celtic Tiger is a powerful animal that frees us from the Catholic Church, and from other traditional constraints: "it tears asunder the motley ties that have bound us . . . it strips off halos . . . profanes all that is holy, leaving no other nexus between man and man than naked self-interest and callous cash payment" (Marx and Engels, 1985: 82). Material affluence provides the structural conditions that make it possible to reject the older religion and to expose the systematic culture of power abuse and cruelty at the heart of institutional Irish Catholicism. Simultaneously, the new materialism provides the medium and the "register" for recompense and atonement: compensation, cash settlements. Victims of child sexual abuse and cruelty sue the Church for financial compensation. In this we can identify the collisions of diverse social forms in the very contemporary and global political culture of juridification and victimology; specifically, modern possessive individualism and rationalised acquisitiveness in the calculated pursuit of money, legitimated in the name of the traditional values of making atonement and restoring community.

The overdetermined, divergent, paradoxical and ambivalent meanings condensed in the Celtic Tiger as a collective representation of identity in the collision cultures of contemporary Ireland is a classic symptom of anomie (Durkheim, 1984, 1966), the condition of normative confusion resulting from the eclipse of a singular hegemonic source of moral authority, and the emergence of a wide variety of moral scripts competing for legitimacy. This proliferation of divergent vestigial and emergent moral scripts, collectively represented by the Celtic Tiger, reflects a deeper fragmentation of the social and political imaginary, a mutation of the symbolic order as such; a symbolic mutation of the same order of magnitude and significance for understanding contemporary Irish culture and identity as LeFort's (1988) identification of the empty place of power marked by the French and American revolutions, or as Durkheim identifies at a deeper level than the Reformation, a whole sea-change taking place in early modern society of which the disagreement in Faith marked by the Reformation is only symptomatic: economic changes in the division of labour, and the accompanying transformation of the form of social integration from mechanical to organic solidarity; the emergence of the individual and the decline of the group, and the transformation of collective representations and moral authorities from religious to social. Similarly, the fundamental mutations of the symbolic order that are the deep sources of the culture and identity of the Celtic Tiger are not to be found within the national society, but are symptomatic of the civilisational sea-change of twenty-first-century globalisation.

CHAPTER 8

Millenarianism and Utopianism in the New Ireland: The Tragedy (and Comedy) of Accelerated Modernisation

I N BERMAN'S *ALL THAT IS SOLID MELTS INTO AIR: The Experience of Modernity*, he describes our experience of modernity as that of perpetual change and transformation; we are caught up and buffeted around by the ambivalent and contradictory forces which we set in motion but do not control.

> There is a mode of vital experience — experience of space and time, of the self and others, of life's possibilities and perils — that is shared by men and women all over the world today. I will call this body of experience "modernity". To be modern is to find ourselves in an environment that promises us adventure, power, joy, growth, transformation of ourselves and the world — and, at the same time, that threatens to destroy everything we have, everything we know, everything we are. Modern environments and experiences cut across all boundaries of geography and ethnicity, of class and nationality, of religion and ideology: in this sense modernity can be said to unite all mankind. But it is a paradoxical unity, a unity of disunity: it pours us all into a maelstrom of perpetual disintegration and renewal, of struggle and

contradiction, of ambiguity and anguish. To be modern is
to be part of a universe in which, as Marx said, "all that
is solid melts into air" (Berman, 1983: 15).

Developing Berman's theme, other authors have described
the contemporary zeitgeist as "late-modern" (Bauman, 1993)
emphasising the intractability of modernity's ambivalence and
paradox, or "post-modern" (Jameson, 1991) pointing to the
intensification of the experiences of social fragmentation and
individuation, the continuation of modernity, but without the
utopian hopes and dreams that made the experience bearable.
Beck, Giddens and Lash (1994) use the concept of "reflexive
modernisation" to describe an acceleration of the processes
of transformation in contemporary society, intensifying and
accentuating the experiences Berman describes in a second-
wave of modernity, driven by the generation of risk and the
unforeseeable consequences of technological development. In
addition, all of these authors, Bauman (1998), Beck (2000),
Giddens (1999), Jameson (2000), have used the term "globalisation" to reiterate the transnational, world-scale nature of
these collective social historical experiences, experiences that
are "shared by men and women all over the world today".

We in Ireland are also caught up in these world historical
processes of modernisation and experiences of modernity,
albeit modulated and mediated by our own histories, our own
insertion into the global political economy, and our own particular experiences as members of different socio-economic
classes, religious and political persuasions, as men and women,
as urban and rural dwellers, as native born and as newcomers,
as Travellers and minorities. Furthermore, the unprecedented
economic boom of the mid-1990s, the period of the so-called

"Celtic Tiger", short-lived, uneven in its effects, unstable and insecure, has amplified and exacerbated the experiences of accelerated modernisation. We are caught up in a world historical process. Abstract forces of modernisation/globalisation, like fate and destiny, appear to us as metaphysical as we seem to have no control over them. We are obliged to participate in this process: we are forced "on pain of extinction" to adapt to the new mode of civilisation (Marx, 1985: 84). As Walter Benjamin puts it, the tragedy of development is that "we are propelled along the road to catastrophe". We cannot foresee this, Benjamin says; we can only see retrospectively the damage already done as we are thrown backwards into the future: "The Angel of History stares in horror at a pile of debris heaping up before him as he is propelled backwards by a storm blowing out of heaven. This storm is what we call Progress" (Benjamin, 1992: 249).

The Faustian Tragedy of Development

One of the most perceptive accounts of the deep origins of the experience of modernity is the epic of Faust by the German poet/philosopher Goethe. Berman (1983) shows how Goethe's tragic story of Faust is the prototypical formulation of the paradoxes of modernity and modernisation, which, though written in the late eighteenth and early nineteenth century is still pertinent to Irish experiences today. In Goethe's epic, when the devil first tries to tempt Faust, he finds that Faust's wants are not the usual fare of money, power and sexual conquest that the devil deals in. Sure, I would like these, Faust says, but these are merely means to greater ends, means to satiate desires that are higher, deeper, and altogether infinitely more expansive; desires that are both subtle and gross, for experiences that are intense and painfully excessive. What I want, Faust says, is to embody and experience the universe of human potential. He says to the devil:

> Do you not hear? I have no thought of joy!
> The reeling whirl I seek, the most painful excess
> Enamoured hate and quickening distress
>   . . . My mind
> Shall not henceforth be closed to any pain, and what is
>   portioned out to all mankind,
> I shall enjoy deep within myself, contain within my spirit
>   summit and abyss,
> pile on my breast their agony and bliss,
> and let my own self grow into theirs unfettered
> 'Til as they are, I too, at last, am shattered.

Like Goethe's Faust, many of the actors in the contemporary Irish tragedy of development are driven by noble aspirations and high ideals. Our Faustian desire for development is not just for wealth, but for the freedom from want that wealth can bring about: freedom from ignorance, and also from innocence; freedom of experience and expression; riches of knowledge, cultural and emotional development; a quest for transformative experience, of ourselves, of others, of the world. This utopian dream is ambivalent and paradoxical: it is both emancipatory and megalomaniacal, for the price we pay for exercising will and consciousness is that we become subject to our power over ourselves. As Marx (1985: 86) says, our society, a society "that has conjured up such gigantic means of production and exchange, is like the sorcerer who is no longer able to control the powers of the netherworld whom he has called up by his spells". Although modernisation is foisted upon us from outside by the experience of imperialism and colonisation, and in a post-colonial era through exogenous forces of globalisation, we should not delude ourselves, as we so often do, that we are innocent victims of history. We are like Faust: the desire for development is our own desire, and that desire is for full and unlimited development, wherever it may lead us, even up to and including our own self-destruction. As Berman says, "The deepest horrors of Faustian development spring from its most honourable aims and its most authentic achievements" (Berman, 1983: 72).

Goethe's Faust symbolises the aspirations of modern people for full and unlimited development and their often terrible and beautiful unforeseeable consequences. Homer Simpson sells his soul for a doughnut to the devil in the form of Ned Flanders, and Irish people are at times happy to trade everything, if not for a doughnut then for designer clothes and a dormer bungalow with an unobstructed view. Our public representatives seem like so many cartoons: former Taoiseach Charlie Haughey, the "squireen" with extravagant taste in shirts; former Government Minister Michael Lowry, the price of whose corruption, it seems, was no more than an extension to his house. But collectively, historically, modern people strike a better bargain with the devil. Faust sells his soul for knowledge/power, and this is what his devil, Mephistopheles, grants him, but the catch is — the devil, as always, is in the detail! — that he can never trade them back. Faust becomes damned to perpetual striving. He can never again say: "Ah, linger still! Thou art so fair", or as we might say in our own vernacular idiom: "That's grand now. That'll do fine!" The desires of modern people are insatiable, and as Durkheim (1966) shows "insatiability is a sign of morbidity". Unlimited horizons and insatiable desires are the conditions of egoism, delusions of omnipotence, psychosis (Freud, 1961) and anomie (Durkheim, 1966). The ability to limit ourselves, to govern our individual and collective desires, collides with the Faustian spirit of the Celtic Tiger, whose appetites and desires can know no limit. Though part of us wants to say "hold it there, that'll be alright", another part knows that the cat is out of the bag and we can never again be satisfied with what we have.

Ironically, the Faustian bargain that we made to extricate ourselves from the state of nature throws us back into that same state. The devil wins; we end up in Hell. We are condemned to "a perpetual and restless pursuit of power after power, ceasing only in death" (Hobbes, 1914). Power, which began as a means to an end, is now an end in itself, the only end. Weber's (1972: 71) critique of the irrationalism of rationalised acquisition, Marx's (1985: 82) critique of capitalism's reduction of all value to a "cash nexus", the "bottom line", is that all are forms of modern nihilism, the catastrophe at the end of the road to development. One of the idiomatic expressions of the tragedy of development is apparent in the paradox and ambivalence in the discourse on education in contemporary Ireland, which simultaneously blames, and justifies, the dominance of instrumentality in terms of economic modernisation: e.g. "The role of the university is to provide a suitably qualified workforce so that companies can expand and develop" (UCC President's report 1995–1996), which is in stark contrast with the original pedagogical principles underpinning the National University of Ireland, expressed in J.H. Cardinal Newman's *Idea of a University* wherein he warns that "scientific pedantry fossilises the mind". As Bonner (1998) argues, this problem reflects the eclipse of a moral practical discourse grounded in Catholicism, and its replacing with the moral practical discourse of modernity, namely "excellence" undefined, the nihilistic pursuit of power after power, ceasing only in death. Like children, we may be frustrated when we don't get what we want, but we are frightened when we do. The sense of limitlessness we experience in the moral practical discourse of modernity, wherein there are no limits, and thus nothing against which we reflexively form/condition ourselves as human, produces anomie and egoism (Durkheim, 1966) and is one of the conditions of high rates of suicide amongst young people in contemporary Ireland.

As Berman so eloquently demonstrates through his interpretation of Goethe's *Faust*, modernisation comes at a price: the thorough penetration of the commodity form (Marx), the dominance of instrumental rationality (Weber), the ascendance of individualism and egoism (Durkheim). As a result, the emotional ground tone of contemporary Ireland is ambivalence. We have already made the Faustian bargain, but are still strongly vestigially Catholic and we cannot sin guiltlessly. We walk through the valley of the shadow of death, but without any longer protection from the fear of evil. Free to act on our own individual conscience, rather than have our actions determined by the collective conscience, we find ourselves in that joyous terrible dilemma of Oscar Wilde's: we can resist everything, except temptation. In Berman's account, this dilemma or paradox is captured by the notion that central to modernity is the ambiguous spirit of the devil. On the one hand, Mephistopheles is the personification of evil:

his name spells corruption, destruction, death and decay: Lord of Flies, Prince of Darkness, Father of Lies, with associations of insatiability, lust, envy, pride, gluttony, sloth, avarice, wrath, the seven deadly sins of excess and boundlessness which the children of the Celtic Tiger commit freely and gladly. On the other hand, the devil is the Fallen Angel, Lucifer, the Bearer of Light, the Morning Star, who does the work of God and has a positive role in creation by paving the way for more creation and redemption through his destruction and corruption. This ancient paradox that lies at the heart of Christian cosmology is fundamental to understanding the zeitgeist of contemporary Ireland.

Part of the tragedy of development in the magical/terrible Faustian world of contemporary Ireland is that innocent victims are swept away, along with old values, inherited traditions, cultures, landscapes, ways of life, crushed under the wheels of progress. But the tragedy also stems from the fact that innocent victims are at times themselves willing and active (if unself-conscious) participants in those very processes of accelerated modernisation that have mortally injured them. The casualties of accelerated modernisation are swept away by a tide of events that they themselves have helped to set in motion.

Ireland's Great Hunger for Development

We can see this deep paradox of modern Irish life in Patrick Kavanagh's poem "The Great Hunger".[1] The deep paradox of the Great Hunger — that is, what is "great" (positive) about the Great Hunger — is that in Lacanian terms it is the

---

[1] "The Great Hunger", in Peter Kavanagh (ed.) (1972), *Patrick Kavanagh: The Complete Poems*, New York, The Peter Kavanagh Hand Press, pp. 79–104.

original collective traumatic experience, the constitutive Lack that makes us what we are.[2] The Famine (in Irish *an Gorta,* meaning "hurt", "injury", "wound") is the collective historical mortal wound that killed Traditional Ireland, and at the same time *an Gorta Mór* — the great wound — is the primal scene of pain, horror and torment that gives birth to Modern Ireland. It is the constitutive moment, the point that collects us as a society: it is the death of the collective mythic Father and Mother, the ancestors from whom we are all descended. It creates and recalls generations of emigration; it collects the Diaspora. It is the great agony that underpins modern Irish religiosity and legitimates the moral authority of the Catholic Church. It collects the various strands of national consciousness, from the lost motherland of romantic sentimentality, to the betrayal of Reason that animates rational Home Rule,[3] to the murderous genocide that must be avenged that has inspired militant Republicanism. The Great Hunger lies at the base and at the heart of modern Ireland. The ambivalence which contemporary Irish people feel towards the Great Famine is apparent in President Mary Robinson's 150th anniversary Famine commemoration as *celebration*: the recollection of the

---

[2] The constitutive Lack is a central Lacanian concept and is present throughout his oeuvre. See for example "In you more than you" in Jacques Lacan (1977), *The Four Fundamental Concepts of Psychoanalysis*, New York, Norton. For a thorough exposition of the theme of the ideological function of the Lack, see also Zizek (1989).

[3] One of the main wellsprings of support for the Liberal parliamentary Home Rule movement in nineteenth-century Ireland was that British administration of Ireland from London was inefficient and irrational. The abject failure of the English government and its offices in Ireland to respond adequately to famine conditions in the 1840s was one of the main proofs of the argument for Home Rule.

Famine became the affirmative moment of historical continuity, and the primal scene of the new birth, a second birth of modern Ireland, the birth of the Celtic Tiger.

Kavanagh's "The Great Hunger", written 100 years after the Famine and 50 years before the birth of the Celtic Tiger, pokes at and reopens this constitutive primal wound by showing how the "great hunger" takes on different forms in changing historical contexts. The Great Hunger is usually taken to refer to the Famine of the 1840s, but for Kavanagh the famine is a spiritual scarcity of Ireland in the 1940s, in twentieth century, modern Ireland. As Kavanagh sees it, the promise of modernity has been broken, and instead of a bright morning, modern Ireland is stagnant and morbid. He depicts the terrible world after independence but when the progress promised by Independence had already become antiquated and ossified. Kavanagh depicts an Ireland that is spiritually stifling, intellectually dead and emotionally crippled; when people lived as modern peasants, more like badgers than like human beings; a world of hunger and scarcity — not just of material poverty in an underdeveloped political economy where people spent a lifetime not living but merely existing, scratching a living from peasant holdings, but of spiritual poverty in an underdeveloped libidinal economy, of emotional and sexual underdevelopment. "Life dried in the veins of these women and men", Kavanagh says. "There is no future but time stretched for the mowing of hay". In this static world a man's act means "nothing, not a damn thing". Ireland is a closed, narrow, parochial world of ignorance and prejudice, where "the chapel pressed its low ceiling" over the bent backs of a servile congregation.

For Kavanagh, the dreamer, the Great Hunger is the expression in his time and place of the modern Irish Faustian desire for change, progress, development. As soon as this process is set in motion and people begin to emerge from the shackles of a world that has become antiquated, the stage is set for an explosive confrontation between modern desires and sensibilities and the old, antiquated and outmoded world. Bearers of avant-garde cultures in backward societies, as Kavanagh was, experience the Faustian split with particular intensity. Their inner anguish has often inspired revolutionary visions, actions and creations, and no doubt this is the fissure that produced talents ranging from Joyce to U2, from Flann O'Brien to Brian Friel. That Westlife or Maeve Binchy should be seen to be the bearers of this torch should be a cause for concern, as it may well herald that what was fraught, and fecund, in Irish culture, is becoming scarred over, dead, and insensitive.

But as people are torn and tear themselves free from traditional worlds, they are also free to fall in love with them again. The new virility, liveliness, awakening, that accompanies the lifting of traditional morality, sexual freedom, hedonism rather than denial of the body and the mortification of the flesh, provokes ambivalence. We are thrilled by the new eroticism evident for the first time in the reawakened, reworked, and reinvigorated traditional content of *Riverdance*. When freed from tradition, we gain the ability to see good in it — integrity, solidity, stability, continuity, groundedness. This nostalgia for a lost world is very obviously the basis of the emigrants' desire and romantic yearning, but it is also the basis of the modern continentals' interest in rural Ireland. The modern metropolitan who would, as it were, trade in his cosmopolitan worldliness for a quiet retreat in the west of Ireland, where he fantasises that the authentic, the pure, somehow still resides: New Age Travellers in West Cork and East Clare, spiritual refugees from post-industrial society; cynical, disillusioned Germans who came to Ireland in search of authenticity, but who were let down by the modernity of the natives they hoped would be naïve, and are now too long gone from German industry to get back into the business; Dubliners who become chronic "weekenders", in Galway, Westport, Clifden, pushing westwards until they fall into the Atlantic, or exhausted from the long drive, collapse in the door of the suburban house in the private development of exclusive holiday homes that they've relocated from Dublin to Achill Island. In this movement, Marx (1985: 84) says, peasants are "rescued from the idiocy of rural life" and metropolitans force villagers "to adopt what it calls civilisation into their midst". Rural community declines and is erased by development, and is then rebuilt by nostalgic lifestyle warriors, settlers on new internal frontiers in villages along the west coast build a simulacrum of a "traditional" village community, a superficial copy of an original that perhaps never existed.

Asymmetrical love affairs between worldly metropolitans and innocent (or at least what are imagined to be innocent) country folk frequently end in disillusionment and tragedy. During the 1970s and 1980s, the tiny village of Doolin on the west coast of Clare became the object of desire for modern urbane Irish people and continentals, who imagined that they saw in its pubs, its musicians and "local characters", something essential, authentic, which, if they could get close to it and possess it, might save them from transcendental homelessness, the spiritual vacuity, cultural amnesia and loss of particularity characteristic of modern life. Within a short time, the car park at Gussie O'Connor's pub was crowded with Dublin- and EU-registered cars; 15- and 20-roomed bed and breakfasts, Tourist Board Approved, hot and cold TV *en suite*, all mod cons, bourgeoned like mushrooms on horse manure as investors and locals cashed in on the interest. The biggest mod con turned out to be the complete destruction of the original cherished object. Doolin was emptied out of any particular local content, characters elevated to minor celebrities, only to be discarded as fashions changed, and small farmers transformed into petty-bourgeois hoteliers, speculators and property developers. After the brief but intense fling, Doolin is left today a tawdry, desolate, debauched cultural wasteland. "The good is gone out of it", people say, a pithy figure of speech that applies to so much in Ireland today. The epitaph to a life ruined by modern black magic is graffiti on a toilet door of a Doolin pub: "Musicians make millionaires out of publicans, and publicans make alcoholics out of musicians".

Goethe's Faust has three incarnations: the Dreamer, the Lover and the Developer. Kavanagh represents the Faustian incarnation of the Dreamer. He expresses the hunger and dreams for development, affluence, and the power and freedom that accompany them, that lies in the hearts of modern Irish people — desires that are intolerable to repress, but when released are insatiable and impossible to fulfil and end in death and catastrophe. The nativist settlers on the internal frontier who search for the vestiges of traditional Ireland — the imaginary "Real" Ireland of the post-Hinde 1980s postcard — represent Faust's incarnation as the Lover, who romanticises and yearns for a lost innocence. But the Real Ireland of the postcard is the Lacanian "Real": the void in the symbolic order of modern Ireland, into which the lover projects his own romantic fantasy, and through pursuing the fantasy of the Real, succeeds only in destroying the imagined thing he thought he loved.

Irish incarnations of the Developer are similarly fraught with tragedy. Goethe's Faust becomes the Developer when he turns his attentions away from romance, the pursuit of pleasure and experience, to the transformation of the material world, and he systematically sets about building an enormous commercial enterprise. He pursues his own desires for wealth, power and fame, but in so doing it has the consequence of transforming — for better and for worse — the lives of others around him. Some are bulldozed out of the way, but many others become employees and collaborators and find vitality and meaning through their activity. Idleness is transformed into thriving enterprise, waste ground bristles with new houses and communities, and bustles with business. Contemporary Ireland is swarming with Developers, and we celebrate and idealise dream development projects like Dublin's Temple Bar as material evidence of the Faustian self-transformation of our society and portents of what we may do in the future.

Such a Faustian Irish developer is Brendan O'Regan. Beginning as a caterer to transatlantic flights refuelling at Foynes in the 1950s, O'Regan initiated the world's first Duty Free airport shop. Later at Shannon he developed the world's first tax free export processing zone, an initiative that has since become not only the cornerstone of Ireland's economic development strategy over the past fifty years, but has become a model for economic modernisation and development throughout the world. In addition, O'Regan initiated the restoration of Bunratty and other castles and national historical and heritage sites. A key adviser to Lemass, the Taoiseach who oversaw the end of protectionism and the opening of the Irish economy in the 1960s, O'Regan has been a leader driving industrial and tourism development in Ireland for half a century. At least two generations and several hundreds of thousands of Irish people directly and indirectly owe their present affluence and prosperity to his vision and energy. In addition to his role in economic modernisation, in the 1980s at the height of the conflict in Northern Ireland, O'Regan founded Co-operation North to foster cross-border community relations. O'Regan's life's work is that of a true Faustian developer: his goal has been not simply profit as personal gain, but moreover, in so doing, to transform and to improve the world for a broader public, to whom he remains largely unknown.

But Irish developers and their schemes are mostly pseudo-Faustian opportunists and speculators exploiting the moment for a strictly personal profit, rather than, as Faust is, committed to a life-long quest to transform the world and everyone in it and to build a future for all. Johnny Ronan, the brash young would-be Faust driving the Spencer Dock project in Dublin, is a typical Irish Developer: the son of a farmer who moved to the city whose vision of the city remains that of a farmer in its sense of space.[4] His Spencer Dock proposal is for a vast groundscraper taken from a catalogue of global "anywhere architecture", masked with the façade of a conference

---

[4] For a full account of Dublin's developer culture, see Frank McDonald (2000), *The Construction of Dublin*, Dublin, Gandon.

centre by a celebrity architect, concerned solely with exploiting to an absolute maximum the rentable square footage of
office space. An older, mature Faust is represented by a
builder whose construction company has become practically
synonymous with suburban housing development in Ireland, a
giant man whose huge hands and lined face tell of a youth of
physical labour as he built his empire up through lean years.
This Colossus sat through a meeting of architects, planners
and citizens convened by Cork City Hall to share views on the
future development of their city. Dreams and schemes and
talk of the future ground to a halt when the Developer inter-
jected, stating: "Whatever about what the city needs, I'll tell
you what people want. They want a three-bedroomed semi-
detached house on a nice estate in the suburbs, with a patch
of grass front and back. That's what they want, and that's what
I'll give them." Irish pseudo-Faustian developers aspire to being high-flying global visionaries, but their visions are still
bounded by the farmyard gate and the parish pump.

The globalisation of Irish culture by Irish cultural developers and entrepreneurs all too often produces cultural homogenisation that reduces Irish culture and identity to a re-
petitive, simplistic formula easily consumed on the global
market. Oscar Wilde famously said, "We are all in the gutter,
but some of us are gazing at the stars", by which he meant
that what distinguishes visionary leaders from the ordinary
masses is idealism. The Irish pseudo-Faustian developer is the
inverse of this, and represents the disparagement of idealism
and the cynical debasement of action to the lowest common
denominator. A prominent Irish culture industry developer,
Louis Walsh, exemplifies the thorough penetration of the

commodity form that globalisation entails, and the concurrent emptying-out of any creative impulse from visionary ideals. Walsh, originally from rural Mayo, moved to Dublin, began his career as a booking agent for showbands on the circuit of dancehalls in Irish provincial towns, and in the 1990s developed boy-bands Boyzone and Westlife. Walsh's vision is unabashedly cynical: "Catching sight of East 17 and Take That, he made the obvious observation: They're getting away with it. Why can't we? The next step was Boyzone." His products are import substitutes of the global culture industry, in the same way as Supermacs (founded by a schoolteacher from a nearby small town in county Galway) copies a product formula to substitute McDonalds. Boyzone, Walsh says "are past their 'sell-by' date", but "Samantha Mumba could be the next Jennifer Lopez, Omera Mumba is the Irish Michael Jackson". Like Ronan, and a cohort of pseudo-Faustian businessmen-heroes of the Celtic Tiger, true to Wilde's definition of the cynic as "one who knows the price of everything, but the value of nothing", Walsh says: "I'm not interested in what people think. I just do what I do and it's very successful."[5]

The Paradoxical Idiosyncrasies of Irish Corruption

The paradoxical unity of the global and the local, modernity and tradition in the Irish experience of accelerated modernisation is vividly expressed in the series of public inquiries into political corruption and tax dodging. The Tribunals of Inquiry are expressions of the function of the modern democratic state to equalise consumption through public taxation and a

---

[5] Louis Walsh "The Starmaker", interview, *RTÉ Guide*, 21 April 2001.

regulatory framework, and thus are the very models of modernisation: the formal equality of all citizens before the Law in a bureaucratically integrated administrative system based on principles of legal-rational authority (Weber, 1978). Simultaneously, they function as witch-hunts, belonging to a traditional form of life, in which certain individuals are scapegoated and sacrificed as vessels of the sins of the many to assuage collective guilt and thus to enable us to carry on sinning. In this way the public interest, and the public disinterest, in the Ansbacher lists,[6] and the scandalously extravagant lifestyle of former Taoiseach C.J. Haughey, can be understood in terms of ambivalence. Simultaneously, people are "outraged", and yet have a sneaking regard for Haughey and the Golden Circle. The collective sentiment is as much a mixture of envy and admiration of their audacity, and, as well, a rationally grounded democratic egalitarian desire for justice.

Corruption in public life in Ireland can be seen as an idiomatic expression of the rationalisation of acquisitiveness after Weber's (1976) *Protestant Ethic*, in that it is a unique and peculiar combination of modern rationalisation and pre-modern nepotism. On the one hand, Irish political corruption takes on its own unique form as a legacy of its post-Catholic and postcolonial heritage. The aspect of political corruption in Ireland that shows it to be truly Irish, is, paradoxically, its pettiness or what Nietzsche (1986: 43) would call its mediocrity, for it is constrained and limited by its traditional moral

---

[6] The names of Irish businessmen and politicians who held offshore accounts in the Cayman Islands with the Ansbacher Bank in which profits (frequently generated in the black or grey economy) were channelled to illegally avoid taxation.

inheritance to a narrowly selfish hedonism rather than expressing grandiose, expansionist, boundless vision of the
Ubermensch. To Nietzsche, gluttony, avarice, envy, lust, sloth,
pride and wrath are the seven deadly sins of traditional Chris-
tianity, deadly because their potential for limitlessness, their
boundless, insatiable excess, fundamentally threaten the
moral constraints that form the parameters of traditional
community. Nietzsche approved of such sins, as they can rup-
ture traditional morality and thus unleash the energies of the
future — but only if pushed to the limit; otherwise they are
simply mediocre. The cultural manifestation of this occurred
in the Expressionist movement, Dadaism, etc. As Nietzsche
says of the "ultimate man" who retains a limited vision and
practice in his excess, the "ground-fleas" that embody the
spirit of modern nihilism, "even in your sinning you are mediocre!" (Nietzsche, 1986: 43).

From a Nietzschean point of view, the sins of Irish politicians are abject and venial; they are not the destructive/
heroic sins of the *Ubermensch*, the man of tomorrow. Some,
like Haughey, merely ape the lifestyle of a debauched minor
aristocracy: a mansion, horses, a yacht, sex, drink and expensive clothes. Most are "gombeen men". The gombeen man
(from *gaimbín* (Ir.) interest on a loan, from Middle English
cambia, exchange, barter, from Latin *cambium*) is a village usu-
rer, usually a shopkeeper, publican, merchant or estate agent,
a native Irish petty bourgeois. The Irish socialist leader James
Connolly fought in the 1916 Rising against British imperialism,
but in *The Re-Conquest of Ireland* (1915) he indicts the gombeen men as the real enemy. The gombeen men were land
grabbers and opportunists who fattened on evictions and

emigration, paying tenants' rents over their heads and appropriating their holdings; profiteers who made their fortunes as middle men, hoarding food and grain during the Famine; publicans who set up shop adjacent to Public Works and Relief projects, as payment stations *cum* shebeens and taverns, to relieve the destitute of their relief. Their vice is money grubbing and petty avarice. These gombeen men, Connolly says, "from their position in the country towns, their ostentatious parade of religion and their loud-mouthed assertions of patriotism", were the dominant influence in the national parties. They still constitute the political class in Ireland at the turn of the twenty-first century.

The mediocrity of the sins of Irish politicians reveals the mediocrity of their dreams: their dreams/sins are not expansive, ambitious or inclusive, or based on a calculated desire for gain for all in the future, but rather are oriented towards immediate gratification, purely personal gain. The characteristic moral pathology is not megalomania but mediocrity; not, for example, the substitution of the singularity of the Leader's will for the ideal of a plural, differentiated modern public — this was the great crime of Hitler, Stalin, Amin, Milosevic. Irish political crime is not megalomania and mass murder but petty theft, the use of public office for private gain.[7] The former crimes make history; they become watersheds of revolutionary transformation. The latter un-make history; they

---

[7] Even the sums of money involved — cash payments of tens and occasionally hundreds of thousands of pounds — are small by international comparison of political corruption. Though no doubt the profits made by the corruptors, those developers and businessmen heroes of the Celtic Tiger who paid for political favours, run to hundreds of millions of pounds, these people generally remain immune from investigation and prosecution.

make a moribund stasis. This is evidenced by the tendency of the Tribunals of Inquiry not to generate debate by articulating and interrogating the corruption of collective ideals under-pinning Irish public life, but merely gossip, by concentrating on the "scandal" of individual private conduct.

The Irish Apocalypse, and Intimations of Redemption

In the pre-modern cosmology of traditional Irish Catholicism, the interior that matters is the interior of the soul. In modern Irish consumerism, it is the interior of the house. Walter Benjamin (1999) says, "The bourgeois interior is a dialectical image in which the reality of industrial capitalism is repre-sented visibly." For Benjamin, the combination of clutter and fastidiousness characteristic of the late-nineteenth-century living room was symptomatic of the crisis of overproduction at the heart of modern society, reproduced in the microcosm of the interior as a hysterical cycle of production and con-sumption. James Joyce's interiors in *Dubliners* (1976), espe-cially and typically in the stories "The Sisters", "The Boarding House", "Clay" and "The Dead", are interiorised microcos-mic representations of paralysis, darkness and death, the closed inner worlds characteristic of Dublin crushed and squeezed by the British Empire, the Holy Catholic Church, Nationalism, and commercialism.

The bourgeois interior is "apocalyptic", Benjamin (1999) says. The "apocalypse" means to "open the curtains", to "re-veal" the end of things, the final judgement. Hence, in the Bi-ble, the Apocalypse is the Book of Revelations. By this anal-ogy Benjamin means that written in the interior of the mod-ern home is a cryptic eschatology and teleology of modernity.

By a cultural analysis that Benjamin likens to detective work, a "hermeneutics of the profane", and "a physiognomy of the interior", we can find "traces", clues that foretell the end of modern forms of life. By the eschatological and teleological "ends" of modern life, Benjamin means the goals it strives towards, that, when achieved or fully realised, mark the End: Hell and damnation, but also the possibility of salvation and rebirth. The damnation(s) foretold for modernity which Benjamin has in mind here are various forms of nihilism — the reduction of all value to cash (Marx); the iron cage of rationalised acquisitiveness, wherein the pursuit of wealth stripped of higher religious goals and resting on mechanical foundations becomes a form of mechanised petrification (Weber); the egoistic anti-social cult of the individual (Durkheim). If we take the Irish interior as such a microcosm of dialectical images that reveals the nihilistic pathologies of the broader social metempsychosis, what clues can we find that in their ends (their goals) are revealed the ends of contemporary forms of Irish life, and the end of Irish history?

The playwright Martin McDonagh provides a paradigmatic representation of the interior of the Irish house as dialectical image indexing the pathologies of contemporary Ireland. *The Lonesome West* is set in a contemporary kitchen in Connemara, the *locus classicus* of the Irish spirit in the symbolic order and imaginative structure of Irish culture and identity. Connemara is the heartland of traditional Ireland, as it is where the Irish survived, having been cleared and beaten westwards — "to Hell or to Connaught"; a heartland romantically imagined by Irish revivalists and global primitivists, but in reality a vast refugee settlement, filthy, hungry, teeming, demoralised, seething with resentment and violence. This is the kitchen of contemporary culture represented by McDonagh. The *mise-en-scène* consists of condensed hybrid fusions of forms of life from dialectically opposed worlds: traditional and modern, global and local. Two bachelor brothers, brutish Coleman who has murdered his father, and avaricious Valeen, who blackmails Coleman to sign over his inheritance, occupy the house. The light is dim, though there is a profusion of electrical outlets and power-points, their orange "live" lights glowing with potent malevolence.[8] Modernisation has been through here and has left its mark, but the old hobgoblins are still alive too. Though meanly furnished, it is untidy; the most prominent objects amongst the clutter are old religious icons juxtaposed uneasily with new and spotless appliances; these objects — religious and commodity fetishes — and the antithetical forms of life that they represent — traditional religious and secular modern — are locked in conflict in the Irish interior.

The material and libidinal economy of the household circulates between the claustrophobia of community, family, Catholic sexual morality, and modern materialism, commodity fetishism — the brothers' neurotic fixations on a fashionable shirt and a hair-do, plastic holy statuettes, new kitchen appliances. The drama unfolds as an endless and pointless exchange: of insults between the two equally frustrated and impotent bachelor brothers who homophobically call each other "virgin gay-boys"; of *vol-au-vents* pilfered from wakes, weddings and local community functions, traded for Tayto

---

[8] Although not part of McDonagh's original set directions, this has become a common feature of subsequent productions.

crisps and *poitín*, the commerce between the global and the local represented in their barest meanness and excess. The tragedy is that action is frozen; colliding forms of life are locked in static conflict, generating murder and suicide. There is no transcendence, no redemption, no third moment of dialectical reconciliation, movement or progress in any direction except eternal recurrence, circularity, spiralling downwards into petty recrimination, pointless violence, and meaningless catastrophe. This conflict/stasis of *The Lonesome West* is a metaphor for the interminable cycle of violence and recrimination in Irish history in general, and Northern Ireland in particular. Mirroring the Northern Irish Peace Process, in which politics is the continuation of war by other means, at the end Coleman and Valeen go off to the pub for a drink together, but as they go they are already gathering ammunition for the renewal of hostilities and the continuation of their conflict.

McDonagh's *The Beauty Queen of Leenane* represents the same theme of dialectical conflict degenerated to static eternal recurrence in Irish culture and identity. Again the time/space of the play is an undefined "contemporary" interior, but frozen in an ever-present past. The old mother sits in a rocking chair passively absorbing television. The rocking chair is emblematic of Ireland's paradoxical experience of accelerated modernisation and stasis — in motion, but going nowhere. The formulaic drama of soap opera flickers on the television, reminding us that the stasis of reflexive modernisation is a global problem, albeit accentuated in this local setting. She's just waiting for the news, she says, but it never comes. Time passes, but there is nothing new in Leenane. The interior of the house in Leenane represents continuity despite apparent transformation. The walls are adorned with icons in niches, both sacred and profane. Statuettes of the Virgin, a framed portrait of JFK and Bobby, the Irish American Holy Family, a flashy radio tape deck plays schmaltzy modern Irish traditional muzak, the television soaps are Australian. The mother's daughter/carer/bonded labourer, is depressive, on the threshold of old maidenhood with frustrated dreams of marriage and escape. Electrical conduit runs around the walls, terminating in power points with glowing "live" lights. This is an old Irish home, a traditional house rewired. But modernity is an overlay, tacked on, not fully integrated. A chip pan stands on the electric cooker. Sickening fast food deadening the life process, clogged arteries, obesity, sluggishness. Their diet is Irish fast food: Complan, tea and fancy biscuits — fats and sugar. The house reeks of the mother's urine. She deliberately neglects her infection to annoy her daughter by reminding her of infirmity, decrepitude and death. Her cruelty is reciprocated: Boiling fat from the chip-pan is used to torture, and eventually murder the domineering mother. But even matricide is not enough to break the tortuous stasis. Escape to Boston is the Beauty Queen of Leenane's psychotic delusion, and she eventually takes her mother's place rocking in the chair in front of the television.

That the comedy duo of Pat Short and John Kenny, D'Unbelievables, produced McDonagh's *The Lonesome West* is perfectly apt, as McDonagh's work is black tragicomedy, and their own comedy played on the grotesque tragic and darkly comic forms that are produced by cultural collisions: vanishing giants and trolls from our collective cultural childhood; the fanatically parochial GAA coach; the sadistic and fatherly schoolmaster; the gombeen man — the obsequious "cute hoor" local county councillor with his eye on the Dáil seat. But the utopian gesture of D'Unbelievables is that these social types who embody divergent tendencies of contemporary Irish culture that we hate and love, and love to hate, are also hilarious caricatures, exaggerated to absurdity. The target of comedy, Samuel Johnson says, is "the bad humour of the Father that keeps us in a state of bondage", that makes us slaves to the conventions of his house.[9] D'Unbelievables targeted such "Fathers": priests, teachers, guards, councillors and minor "offeecials" of all sorts, the "little men" who constitute authoritarian and totalitarian forms of life. Freud says that comedy targets "people and objects that lay claim to authority and respect and are in some sense sublime. The degradation of the sublime allows one to have an idea of it as though it were something commonplace, in whose presence I need not pull myself together, but may, to use the military formula, 'stand easy'" (Freud, 1981: 261–2). The double action of comedy, according to Freud, is that it frees us from the tyranny of the Father, but without "killing the Father". Through comedy, we renegotiate our relations with cultural authorities; we try to come to new terms with our inherited traditions. D'Unbelievables' comedy enables us to simultaneously free ourselves from the life-worlds where priests, schoolmasters and "minor offeecials" wield power, and simultaneously allow us to remember fondly those worlds as real and meaningful. The interiors and dream sequences constructed by D'Unbelievables — ideal homes and fantasy dream sequences

---

[9] Johnson, cited in Corrigan (1981).

used in TV ads for the National Lottery — satellite dishes made out of wheelbarrows propped outside red-brick, palisaded, galvanised-roofed monster houses; de Valeraesque comely maidens chasing through meadows with a hurley stick in a surreal fantasy of a feminised, eroticised GAA-meets-*Riverdance* scenario — comes very close to capturing the bizarre imaginative structure of the current Irish phantasmagoria: elements drawn incongruously from the symbolic registers of the traditional and the modern, the local and the global, dialectical images juxtaposed in an extravagant pastiche of hyper-real, post-modern contemporary Ireland.

Kenny and Short say that their comedy is inspired by the forms of life they are familiar with in Ireland's "in-between" towns (Kenny and Short are from middling-sized towns in county Limerick, in-between the city and the country, the global and the local), places all over Ireland living through the experience of accelerated social change as well as the persistence of older forms of life; the same theatres of acceleration, stasis, and cultural collisions where other young people, unable to laugh, or to laugh any longer, choose instead to cry and to die. D'Unbelievables used to test their new material in theatres in county towns, Tralee, Kilmallock, Tuam, before staging them in Dublin, saying that if they found resonance with audiences there, then they knew it would work in Dublin. In other words, the secret of D'Unbeliveables' comedy is not that a city audience laughs at a caricature of a rural Other, as North American and Continental comedy plays with the radical alterity of the Bumpkin, the Peasant, or the Hillbilly. In Irish comedy the rural Other is close to us and familiar: we are laughing at, and with, an aspect of ourselves.

A large proportion of the population in Dublin is from the rural hinterland, and those that are not are intimately, nostalgically connected with it, as the symbolic order and imaginative structure of contemporary Ireland is still very much rural.

Comedy has two distinct moments: a critical disruptive moment that frees its audience from the tyranny of the dominant culture, lets us see the absurdity of the in-between culture that is our *habitus*; and it also has an affirmative moment: that as it estranges us from our *habitus* it also simultaneously reconciles us with that world as familiar and continuous. In Ireland we need both, and the comedic art of Kenny and Short throws open the grotesque horrors of accelerated modernisation in contemporary Ireland, and simultaneously gives us the gift of laughter that shows colliding worlds — traditional and modern, global and local, past and future — in moments of fleeting reconciliation. As *Father Ted* also did, Kenny and Short show us that what is unbelievable about contemporary Ireland is that people manage to live enjoyably in the liminal in-between spaces typical of a strange and paradoxical world in which Irish people presently find ourselves.

Conclusion

As we have shown above, the experience of modernity and modernisation in contemporary Ireland is illustrative of the end of history as interpreted by the Hegelian/Marxist dialectic, and its decomposition into eternal recurrence and stasis, a Nietzschean/Weberian end of Irish history. But, Beck (1994: 32) asks, what of other possibilities? What has becomes of politics — "the art of making oneself at home in the maelstrom, as Marshall Berman put it so nicely"?

The development of contemporary Irish society is charac-terised by increasing fragmentation and individuation, but these processes themselves are historical and social (that is to say collective) experiences, experiences that cut across differences of class, gender, ideology, region and so on. Indi-viduation and fragmentation of collective identities are per-ceived from within the interpretive horizons of particular life-worlds to be unique and irreducible and entirely different from others' experiences. But that perception is itself a social phenomenon, and one with profoundly political implications to boot. It was Margaret Thatcher who said, "There is no such thing as society. There are individual men and women, and there are families."

One of the great dangers facing those of us who are in-terested in a politics that would make us more at home in the maelstrom of accelerated modernisation, that would as Marx says help us to "make our own history with will and consciousness" rather than have it simply happen upon us, is that the scepticism towards unifying projects and the empha-sis on identitarian politics eschews the notion of collective experiences, the interdependency of identities, the reciproc-ity of their material and symbolic exchanges, and even of so-ciety as such. Against this, we hold to the notion that there are experiences that are highly generalised and dispersed and that are shared — perhaps not by everybody, and certainly not experienced in precisely the same way by everyone — but generalised nonetheless.

Globalisation, for example, is experienced very differently in New York and Ballyhaunis, but if we want to speak mean-ingfully of the ways in which culture and forms of life in

Ireland are asymmetrically interdependent with political, economic and cultural processes in America, then notions of collective historical experiences of modernisation at a global
level remain essential and indispensable. The effects of "instrumental rationalisation" (the organising principle of discursive practices of individuation and totalisation now operating
at a global level) in contemporary Ireland, for example, are
experienced very differently if you are a 200-acre dairy
farmer applying for an EU milk quota, or a single mother
from Ballyfermot applying for a supplementary welfare allow-
ance, or a Romanian Gypsy applying for asylum. These experiences are starkly differentiated by class, gender, ethnicity,
language, culture, etc. Even the outcome of the cases may be
completely different; one successful, one endlessly frustrated,
one routinely rejected — or indeed perhaps not. But what
collects them? On what basis could we say that they have
something in common? They are all processed by an impersonal legal-rational rule-governed administrative apparatus
called modern bureaucracy. Despite the fragmentation of
identity and the individuation of experience in contemporary
Ireland, Weber gives us a bead on and an understanding of an
experience that is common to the differentiated identities
that constitute modern Irish society.

While recognising the fragmented identities and differentiated experiences of contemporary Irish life, we must retain
the ability to perceive and potentially to recover the basis of
unity in the diversity. Christians used to believe that the basis
of unity in human diversity was the soul. Marxists used to
believe that the basis of unity in diversity was our capacity to
produce, and our relations to the means of production.

Liberals used to believe that the basis for unity was our capacity for reason. Irish and other nationalists used to believe that the basis for unity lay in our shared ethnicity, and so on in the same vein for feminists and a host of Others. And many continue to hold these beliefs as self-evident truths. Against this orthodoxy, and against the position of other contemporary theorists, including Chomsky and Habermas who ground society in the deep structures of communication, the most advanced schools of philosophy today hold that there is no pre-ordained or fundamental ground of social unity. But that is not to say that there is (or are) no unity (or unities). Rather, the point is that whatever unities exist in any society at a particular historical time are solidarities: social and political collective identities whose ideologies are linked together, articulated with one another in ways that are contingent and transitory. "The absence of a ground of the social means that whatever form of social articulation exists is going to be the result of a laborious process of political construction which creates new habits, new forms of thought, new forms of relation between people. It means the creation of a political tradition" (Laclau, 1991: 59).

The painstaking work of bringing together different ideologies and discourses of identity from a great diversity of points on the social fabric of contemporary Ireland is called "hegemony". To engage in hegemonic articulatory practices, to attempt to constitute a solidarity that would formulate values, norms and principles to guide collective action in a time of hyper-individuation and the fragmentation of a political imaginary, to create a new political tradition in Ireland after "the end of Irish history", is to presuppose the possibility of forming a "we". To rhetorically invoke such a collective subject of contemporary Ireland before s/he has appeared on the historical stage is to make such a strategic utopian political assumption. And to provide a critical hermeneutic analysis of the forms of Irish culture under conditions of accelerated modernisation is to contribute towards setting that stage.

Bibliography

Adorno, T. (1994), *The Stars Down to Earth and Other Essays on the Irrational in Culture*, London: Routledge.

Adorno, T. and Horkheimer, M. (1992) [1944], *Dialectic of Enlightenment*, London, Verso.

Allen, K. (2000), *The Celtic Tiger: The Myth of Social Partnership in Ireland*, Manchester: Manchester University Press

Althusser, L. (1984), "Ideology and ideological state apparatuses: notes towards an investigation", in Zizek, S. (ed.) (1995), *Mapping Ideology*, London: Verso.

Bataille, G. (1988), *The Accursed Share: An Essay on General Economy*, New York: Zone.

Baudrillard, J. (1987), *The Ecstasy of Communication*, New York: Semiotext(e).

Baudrillard, J. (1989), *America*, London: Verso

Bauman, Z. (1990), *Thinking Sociologically*, Oxford: Blackwell.

Bauman, Z. (1991), *Modernity and Ambivalence*, Cambridge: Polity.

Bauman, Z. (1998), *Globalisation: The Human Consequences*, Cambridge: Polity Press.

Bauman, Z. (2000), *Liquid Modernity*, Cambridge: Polity Press.

Beck, U. (2000), *What is Globalization?* Cambridge: Polity.

Beck, U, Giddens, A. and Lash, S. (1995), *Reflexive Modernization: Politics, Tradition and Aesthetics in the Modern Social Order*, Cambridge: Polity Press.

Benjamin, W. (1992), *Illuminations*, London: Fontana.

Benjamin, W. (1992), "Theses on the Philosophy of History", in *Illuminations*, London: Fontana.

Benjamin, W. (1999), "The Interior, the Trace" in *The Arcades Project*, Cambridge, Mass.: Belknap/Harvard University Press.

Benjamin, W. (1999), "Paris: Capital of the Nineteenth Century" in *The Arcades Project*, Cambridge, Mass.: Belknap/Harvard University Press.

Berger, P. (1985), *Pig Earth*, London: Chatto & Windus.

Berman, M. (1983), *All That is Solid Melts into Air: The Experience of Modernity*, London: Verso.

Bonner, K. (1997), *A Great Place to Raise Kids: Interpretation, Science, and the Urban–Rural Debate*, Montreal: McGill Queens' University Press.

Bonner, K. (1998), *Power and Parenting*, Montreal, McGill Queens University Press.

Bourdieu, P. (1977), *Outline of a Theory of Practice*, Cambridge: Cambridge University Press.

Bourke, A. (1999), *The Burning of Bridget Cleary*, London: Pimlico.

Connolly, J. (1915), *The Re-Conquest of Ireland*, Dublin (pamphlet).

Corcoran, M. and White, A. (2000), "Irish democracy and the Tribunals of Inquiry", in Slater, E. and Peillon, M. (eds.), *Memories of the Present: A Sociological Chronicle of Ireland, 1997–1998*, Dublin: IPA, pp. 185–196.

Corrigan, R. (ed.) (1981), *Comedy: Meaning and Form*, New York, Harper & Row.

Coser, L. and Rosenberg, B. (eds.) (1965), *Sociological Theory: A Book of Readings*, New York: Macmillan.

Cronin, M. and O'Connor, B. (2003), *Irish Tourism: Image, Culture and Identity*, Clevedon: Channel View Publications.

De Certeau, M. (1984), *The Practice of Everyday Life*, Berkeley: University of California Press.

Dinneen, P. (1927), *Foclóir Gaeilge/Bearla* (Irish/English Dictionary), Dublin: Educational Company of Ireland.

Durkheim, E. (1966) [1897], *Suicide*, New York: Free Press.

Durkheim, E. (1974) [1923], *Sociology and Philosophy*, New York: Free Press.

Durkheim, E. (1982) [1895], *The Rules of Sociological Method*, New York: Free Press.

Durkheim, E. (1984) [1933], *The Division of Labour in Society*, New York: Free Press.

Durkheim, E. (1995) [1912], *The Elementary Forms of Religious Life*, New York, Free Press.

Economic and Social Research Institute (ESRI) (2000), *Bust to Boom? The Irish Experience of Growth and Inequality*, Dublin: ESRI.

Elias, N. (1991), *The Civilizing Process*, London: Blackwell.

Elias, N. (1995) "Technization and Civilization", *Theory, Culture & Society*, Vol. 12, No. 3, 7–42.

Ellmann, R. (1987), *Oscar Wilde*, London: Penguin.

Foucault, M. (1981), *Power/Knowledge: Selected Interviews and Other Writings*, New York: Vintage.

Foucault, M. (1991), *Discipline and Punish: The Birth of the Prison*, London: Penguin.

Freud, S. (1961) [1930], *Civilization and its Discontents*, New York, Norton.

Freud, S. (1963) [1912], *Totem and Taboo*, New York: Norton.

Freud, S. (1976) [1899], *The Interpretation of Dreams*, London: Penguin.

Freud, S. (1981) [1901], *Jokes and their Relation to the Unconscious*, London: Penguin.

Garavan, T. et al. (1997), *Entrepreneurship and Business Start-ups in Ireland*, Dublin: Oak Tree Press.

Geertz, C. (1993) [1972], *The Interpretation of Cultures*, London: Fontana.

Giddens, A. (1971), *Capitalism and Modern Social Theory: An Analysis of the Writings of Marx, Durkheim and Max Weber*, Cambridge: Cambridge University Press.

Giddens, A. (1979), *Central Problems in Social Theory*, London: Macmillan.

Giddens, A. (1984), *The Constitution of Society*, Cambridge: Polity.

Giddens, A. (1995), "Living in a Post-Traditional Society" in Beck, U. Giddens, A. and Lash, S., *Reflexive Modernization: Politics, Tradition and Aesthetics in the Modern Social Order*, Cambridge: Polity, pp. 56–109.

Global Entrepreneurship Monitor (GEM) (2000), *Entrepreneurship in Ireland*, London: London Business School.

Habermas, J. (2001), *The Postnational Constellation*, London: Polity.

Hebdige, Dick (1979), *Subculture: The Meaning of Style*, New York: Routledge.

Heelas, P. (1996), *The New Age Movement*, Oxford: Blackwell.

Hegel, G.W.F. (1977), *The Phenomenology of Spirit*, Oxford: Oxford University Press.

Hetherington, K. (1996), "Identity Formation, Space and Social Centrality", *Theory, Culture and Society*, Vol. 13, No. 4, pp. 33–52.

Hobbes, T. (1914), *Leviathan*, London, J.M. Dent & Sons.

Inglis, T. (1998), *Moral Monopoly: The Rise and Fall of the Catholic Church in Modern Ireland*, second edition, Dublin: UCD Press.

Jameson, F. (1991), *Postmodernism, or the Cultural Logic of Late Capitalism*, Durham, NC: Duke University Press.

Jameson, F. (2000), "Globalization and Political Strategy", *New Left Review*, Vol. 4.

Jay, M. (1973), *The Dialectical Imagination*, Boston: Little, Brown & Co.

Joyce, J. (1976) [1916], *Dubliners*, London: Penguin.

Kavanagh, P. (1972), "The Great Hunger" in P. Kavanagh (ed.) *Patrick Kavanagh: The Complete Poems*, New York: Peter Kavanagh Hand Press.

Kuhn, T. (1970), *The Structure of Scientific Revolutions*, Chicago: University of Chicago Press.

Lacan, J. (1978), *The Four Fundamental Concepts of Psychoanalysis*, New York: Norton.

Lacan, J. (1994), *Speech and Language in Psychoanalysis*, Baltimore: Johns Hopkins University Press.

Laclau, E and Mouffe, C. (1985), *Hegemony and Socialist Strategy*, London: Verso.

Laclau, E. (1991), "God Only Knows", *Marxism Today*, 56–59.

Lee, J.J. (1989), *Ireland 1912–1985: Politics and Society*, Cambridge: Cambridge University Press.

LeFort, C. (1988), *Democracy and Political Theory*, Cambridge: Polity.

Lukacs, G. (1971), *History and Class Consciousness*, London: Merlin.

McDonald, F. (2000), *The Construction of Dublin*, Dublin, Gandon.

McDonagh, M. (1999), *The Leenane Trilogy*, London: Methuen Drama.

McKay, G. (1996), *Senseless Acts of Beauty*, London: Verso.

McLellan, D. (1980), *The Thought of Karl Marx*, London: Macmillan.

Marx, K. (1964), *Early Writings*, Bottomore, T. (ed.), New York: McGraw Hill.

Marx, K and Engels, F. (1985) [1848], *The Communist Manifesto*, London: Penguin.

Mauss, M. (2002) [1954], *The Gift*, London: Routledge.

Mishra, R. (1999), *Globalization and the Welfare State*, Cambridge: Cambridge University Press.

National Roads Authority (1994), *Annual Report*, Dublin: Government Publications Office.

National Roads Authority (1995), *Annual Report*, Dublin: Government Publications Office.

Nederveen-Pieterse, J. (1998), "Hybrid Modernities: Melange Modernities in Asia", *Sociological Analysis*, Vol. 1, No. 3, 75–87.

Nietzsche, F. (1967), *Beyond Good and Evil*, New York: Gateway.

Nietzsche, F. (1986), *Thus Spoke Zarathustra*, London: Penguin.

O'Carroll, J.P. (1987), "Strokes, cure hoors and sneaking regarders: The influence of local culture on political style", *Irish Political Studies* Vol. 8, 71–92.

O'Connor, P. (1999), *Emerging Voices: Women in Ireland Today*, Dublin: Institute for Public Administration.

O'Hearn, D. (1998), *Inside the Celtic Tiger: The Irish Economy and the Asian Model*, London: Pluto.

O'Neill, J. (1985), *Five Bodies: the Human Shape of Modern Societies.* New York: Cornell University Press.

O'Toole, F. (1999), "Introducing *Irelantis*" in S. Hillen, *Irelantis*, Dublin: Irelantis Ltd..

Offe, C. and Ronge, V. (1982), "Theses on the Theory of the State", in Giddens, A. and Held, D. (eds.), *Classes, Power and Conflict*, Los Angeles: University of California Press, 249–256.

Offe, C. (1984), "Ungovernability: On the Renaissance of Conservative Theories of Crisis" in J. Habermas (ed.), *Observations on the Spiritual Situation of the Age*, Boston: MIT Press.

Peillon, M. (1984), "The structure of Irish ideology revisited" in C. Curtin et al. (eds.), *Culture and Ideology in Ireland*, Galway: Galway University Press.

Peillon, M. (2000), "Carnival Ireland", in E. Slater and M. Peillon (eds.), *Memories of the Present: A Sociological Chronicle of Ireland, 1997–1998*, Dublin: IPA, 133–142.

Ross, A. (1991), *Strange Weather: Culture, Science, and Technology in the Age of Limits*, London: Verso.

Ross, A. (1989) (ed.), *Universal Abandon? The Politics of Postmodernism*, Minneapolis: University of Minnesota Press.

Simmel, G. (1971a) [1903], "The Metropolis and Mental Life", in *On Individuality and Social Forms*, D.N. Levine (ed.), Chicago: University of Chicago Press.

Simmel, G. (1971b) [1918], "The Conflict in Modern Culture", in ibid.

Simmel, G (1971c) [1908], "The Stranger", in ibid.

Slater, E. (2000), "When the Local goes Global" in Peillon, M. and Slater, E. (eds.), *Memories of the Present: A Sociological Chronicle of Ireland 1997–1998*, Dublin:: IPA Press.

Smyth, C., MacLachlan, M. and Clare, A. (2003), *Cultivating Suicide: Destruction of Self in a Changing Ireland*, Dublin: The Liffey Press.

Szakolczai, A. (1999), *Reflexive Historical Sociology*, London: Routledge.

Szakolczai, A. (2000), "Experiences and Identity", Working Paper, NUI Cork, Ireland.

Titmuss, R. (1971), *The Gift Relationship: From Human Blood to Social Policy*, New York: Vintage.

Turner, V. (1967), "Betwixt and Between: The liminal period in Rites de Passage", in *The Forest of Symbols*, New York: Cornell University Press.

Turner, V. (1969), *The Ritual Process*, Chicago: Aldine.

Veblin, T. (1994) [1899], *The Theory of the Leisure Class*, London: Dover.

Virillio, P. (1986), *Speed and Politics*, New York: Semiotext(e).

Weber, M. (1976) [1921], *The Protestant Ethic and the Spirit of Capitalism*, New York: Macmillan.

Weber, M. (1978) [1956], *Economy and Society*, Vols. 1 and 2, Berkeley: University of California Press.

Wittgenstein, L. (1958), *Philosophical Investigations*, Oxford: Basil Blackwell.

Wright Mills, C. (1959), *The Sociological Imagination*, Oxford: Oxford University Press.

Zizek, S. (1989), *The Sublime Object of Ideology*, London: Verso.